THINKING ● HISTORY

JON NICHOL

EXPANSION, TRADE AND INDUSTRY

SIMON & SCHUSTER
EDUCATION

Britain 1750 - 1900

Think about the last time you walked down the main street of your local town, city or suburb. If you had done the same walk 100 and 250 years ago, what might you have heard, seen and smelled? How and why did things change? For example, why do some streets and pubs have African and Asian names?

To 'think history' you have to ask such questions and search for answers using your **sources.** History forces you to try and see what life was like in the past and how things have **changed.**

I chose sources **A-D** to suggest **key changes** from 1750 to 1900. **A** is from a textbook I found for pupils of your age written in 1900 - the end date for this History Study Unit. It struck me as a very good source to work from, full of ideas about how the author wanted young people to view their world.

How many clues can you spot in **A-D** which tell you that Britain went through an industrial, a transport, a farming and a social revolution and gained an empire after 1750?

By 1851 more people lived in towns than in the countryside, thousands of steam-driven factories provided work for millions of workers and a network of railways linked most of Britain's towns. All these **changes** still affect where we live, work and go to school, the language we speak and how we think about the world.

❝ The **Industrial Revolution** In the reign of George II most manufactures were carried on by hand labour, and the population of the northern counties was very small. Early in the reign of George III the inventions of Arkwright, Hargreaves, Crompton and Cartwright caused such improvements in machinery (for spinning and weaving cotton) that production was increased a hundredfold. Watt's invention of the steam-engine made it possible to pump the water out of mines, and so the manufacture of iron in the Pennine districts became easier and more profitable. Lancashire and Yorkshire became 'hives of industry', and the north of England is now far more thickly peopled than the south.

The Philanthropic Reforms The mill-system in the Pennine districts was for long left to take care of itself, and the mills were cold in winter, hot in summer, and unhealthy always. Hours of labour were long, little children hardly able to talk were working when they should have been in bed, and accidents from machinery were common.

The English Constitution The English monarchy is a Limited Monarchy ... the chief power lies not with the King but with his ministers. In reality, however, the power of the Sovereign is very great, especially if she is liked and trusted by the nation as was the case with Queen Victoria.

The British Empire The growth of the Empire in the reign of Queen Victoria has been remarkable. [Britain's colonies like to stay tied to England.] At last, in 1899, during the second Boer War, colonies in all parts of the world elected to take part, and over 30,000 men have already fought and marched side by side with Imperial troops, with honour to themselves and profit to England.

General Remarks The telegraph is now in some cases being superseded by the Telephone, by means of which not only can persons talk with each other in distant parts of the same city, but London and Paris are in telephonic communication with each other. ❞ **(A)**

(Roscoe Mongan, *The Oxford and Cambridge History of England from B.C. 55 to A.D.1904,* 1904)

2

Advert!

Weetabix sold a book about the history of Britain with an advert on their cereal packets. In a similar way, you have to prepare a picture advert for *Expansion, Trade and Industry* to go on a cereal packet. The advert should highlight **changes** in Britain from 1750 to 1900. Use sources **A-D** and anything else you can find in this and other books.

1 Studying the sources (AT3, AT2)

Working by yourself or in pairs:

- Note three questions you would like to ask about **B**, and three or more things that you can see happening in the picture. What thoughts or feelings does **B** give you? What message do you think the artist was trying to get across in **B**? What use is **B** as a source to help you learn about factory life?

- You can take the role of a person in **B**, and then the class can interview you about what is going on in the picture.
- What does **C** suggest about how towns have changed between 1750 and today? Would your local town have been like **C**?
- What does **D** tell you about changes in farming?

2 Research (AT3)

Use this and other books and sources to find out how Britain changed from 1750 to 1900, taking the themes (**in bold type**) below.

3 The history advert (AT1)

- Design your advert, using a mix of headlines, pictures and text to make the best-selling impact.
- On your advert draw a picture or describe how things might have changed from 1750 to 1900 for: **dress; transport** - roads and rail; **industry** - factories; **agriculture** - fields and farming; **food and drink; towns** - street life, shops, new buildings; and **other things** that you have found out about such as **kings and queens; wars; inventions.**
- The advert should show that HISTORY IS FUN!
- Put your advert on display. As a class, judge which advert should win the cereal packet advertising contract.

This picture is from a novel written to campaign for better working conditions in factories

Exeter, c.1750

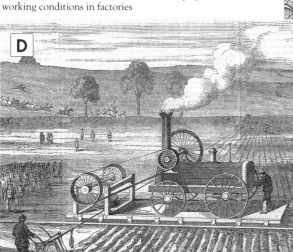

The latest ploughing method, c.1900. How do you think the way fields were ploughed had changed from 1750?

ACTIVITY · ACTIVITY ·

3

Timeline

Next time you go on a bus or car ride, try and guess what **periods** the buildings you pass belong to. When were they built and how old are they? The shape of a building and its doors, windows and roofs are clues as to the period in which it was built. We give the names of our ruling families and their members to these **periods** of history:

Rulers	Period	Other names for period
George II, 1727-60	Georgian	Hanoverian - their family came from Hanover
George III, 1760-1820	Georgian	
George IV, 1820-30	Georgian	Regency (1811-37) George IV had been regent from 1811-20
William IV, 1830-37	Georgian	
Victoria, 1837-1901	Victorian	

The Georgians copied the way the Greeks and Romans built their homes, temples and town halls - we often use the term **classical** to describe it, **A**. The Victorians took their ideas from the Middle Ages and built in the same - Gothic - style, **B**. The Houses of Parliament are our most famous Gothic building. Georgians and Victorians also made their furniture, cutlery and china in the **style** of the **period.**

Timeline!

As a young historian, you can investigate your local area to find out if there are any Georgian and Victorian buildings around.

1 Dating buildings (AT1, AT3)
• Study **A** and **B** and draw up a list of points to help you recognise Georgian and Victorian buildings: shape of building; roof; doors; windows; pillars; decorations.
• Use your list to help you date buildings you pass to and from school, or around where you live. Draw a sketch of a local Georgian and a local Victorian house.

2 House design (AT2)
Design the front of your own Georgian or Victorian house. As a class, you can then hold an architectural competition to see which house is the favourite.

3 Timeline (AT1, AT3)
• Find the houses-for-sale adverts in your local newspaper. Cut them out and put them into three piles - modern, Victorian and Georgian houses. Draw a timeline or a series of columns with headings and stick in your cut-out pictures of the houses.
• You can create a timeline for 1750 to 1900 **either** on your own, using a double page in your book, **or** as a class, by setting up a wall display. Put dates across the top and the four National Curriculum headings (picked out in bold capital letters on the contents page) down the side.

ACTIVITY · ACTIVITY ·

Class and Society in 1750

A

A was an archer,
who shot at a frog;
B was a butcher,
and had a great dog.
C was a captain,
all covered with lace;
D was a drunkard,
and had a red face.
E was an esquire,
with pride on his brow;
F was a farmer,
and followed the plough.
G was a gamester,
who had but ill-luck;
H was a hunter,
and hunted a buck.
I was an innkeeper,
who loved to carouse;
J was a joiner,
and built up a house.
K was King William,
once governed this land;
L was a lady,
who had a white hand.
M was a miser,
and hoarded up gold;

N was a nobleman,
gallant and bold.
O was an oyster girl,
and went about town;
P was a parson,
and wore a black gown.
Q was a queen,
who wore a silk slip;
R was a robber,
and wanted a whip.
S was a sailor,
and spent all he got;
T was a tinker,
and mended a pot.
U was a userer,
a miserable elf;
V was a vintner,
who drank all himself.
W was a watchman,
and guarded the door;
X was expensive,
and so became poor.
Y was a youth,
that did not love school;
Z was a zany,
a poor harmless fool.

Can you think of any nursery rhymes that tell you about life in the past? **A** is a nursery rhyme alphabet for children. In it I hope you can find lots of clues about the jobs people did around 1750. In the 1750s, English society was a pyramid shape with the king at the top. I worked out table **B** from things historians have written about the eighteenth century.

The Nursery Rhyme Pyramid

You can combine sources **A** and **B** to form a pyramid and then write a nursery rhyme about each social layer in your pyramid.

1 Research (AT3)
Find out what you can about the social groups in **A** and any others that you have read about.

2 The pyramid and the nursery rhyme (AT2, AT1)
• On a single or double page draw a pyramid of the groups in **B**.
• For each group, put in the people from **A** who might be in that group.
• Make up a nursery rhyme for one person in each group, similar to any nursery rhymes you know.
• As a class, you can read out your rhymes or you can have a class display of them, or you can look at your pyramids in groups.

B The Social Pyramid, c.1750

Layer	Social rank	Families
1	The Royal Family	1
2	Great Landlords	400
	Wealthy Squires	800
3	Squires	4,000
4	Lawyers	20,000
	Civil Servants	20,000
	Vicars, Priests	30,000
	Merchants	30,000
	Rich Farmers	75,000
5	Shopkeepers, Traders	120,000
6	Servants	750,000
	Craftsmen	180,000
	Farm workers	1,250,000

Adam Smith

Today the Government has economists to help it plan the economy. In 1776 Adam Smith wrote the first modern book on economics, *Wealth of Nations*. In it he gave advice on how to make a country rich. To Adam Smith the key was what we did with our money. **Firstly,** he said we could spend it on buying and selling goods. **Secondly,** cash could be used to make things and to pay for building factories, shops, warehouses, and for improving farming, education and training. **Thirdly,** we could keep our wealth in the bank, or in commodities [things] such as wool, coal, iron-ore, and fruit, vegetables and meat.

Soon after Adam Smith wrote his book the British government sent thousands of convicts to live in Australia, as they could no longer go to America. Map **A** shows a place where they might have settled. The Government hoped that the colonists would be able to grow their own food and make their own goods. After seven years many prisoners would end their sentences and would have to stay in the colony - they had no way of getting home. So a colony would have to plan for the future. Table **B** lists the things that Adam Smith said might make a colony rich.

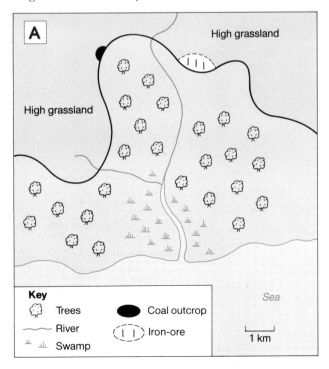

A

High grassland

High grassland

Sea

Key
- Trees
- River
- Swamp
- Coal outcrop
- Iron-ore

1 km

B
1 **Savings and investment** in roads, canals, farms, factories.
2 **Better transport** - turnpike roads instead of dirt tracks, canals instead of rivers.
3 **New ways of farming** to provide food for the factory workers and raw materials for the factories and workshops.
4 **Trade** - money should be spent on advertising, on salesmen and on ships to sell abroad what the colony makes.
5 **Research and inventions** to invent new ways of making things and new goods to sell.
6 **Business** - ambitious businessmen to set up and run firms and factories.
7 **Education** - well-educated and trained bosses and workers.
8 **Population** - a growing population to work and buy goods.
9 **Savings** to invest in **1-8**.

Economic Adviser

How well do you think you might do as an economic adviser to the Government in planning a new colony's economy? Study map **A** closely, and then take the following steps. You can work on your own, in pairs or in threes.

1 The problem (AT1)
You have to draw up a plan to develop the economy of the colony. You have **20 units of money** to invest in ideas **1-9** above, in any other ideas you might have, or to keep back in reserve. Spending is in **whole units.**

2 Research (AT3)
Find out what you can about the ideas in table **B**.

3 Agreement (AT1)
By yourself, or with your partner or group, put the ideas in the order in which you would carry them out, with the money you would spend on each.

4 Class presentation (AT1)
Present your plans to the class, **either** as part of a discussion **or** as a wall poster.

Population Growth

Think of your class as a time machine. The family names of members of your class give us clues as to how people have moved or migrated through time and the jobs they used to do. How many names like Smith or Thatcher tell you about village crafts, many of which have died out? Which names give you an idea about the village, town, area or country where your ancestors came from?

Since 1750 there have been huge changes in the number of people in Britain and where they live and work. Before 1750 Britain was a country of small towns, villages, hamlets and scattered farms. A quote from Michael Reed, a university historian, fills out the picture:

66 *Most towns were very small so that trees, hedges, corn fields, horses and pigs were all very close to people, and the harvest was a matter of serious concern among all ranks of society. Gregory King [a famous economist] thought that there were 794 places in England and Wales deserving to be called towns, but 400 of these had fewer than 700 inhabitants. Less than a quarter of the population lived in towns ... In 1801, out of a total population in England and Wales of 9.25 million, only 17.5% lived in towns with over 20,000 inhabitants.* 99 **(A)**

(Michael Reed, *The Georgian Triumph, 1700-1830*, 1984)

Around 1750 Britain's population began to rise, **B**. No one is sure why, although the birth-rate and a drop in the death-rate, **C**, played a key part.

Factfile **E** gives you some **reasons** or **causes** of the population growth. However, countries like Ireland and Sweden also had the same kind of increase at the same time but they did not go through agrarian, transport and industrial revolutions. How many of the reasons in **E** might apply to them?

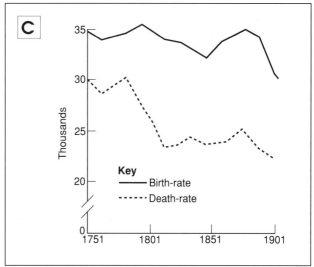

Changes in the birth-rate and death-rate, 1751-1901

The increase in the population of towns

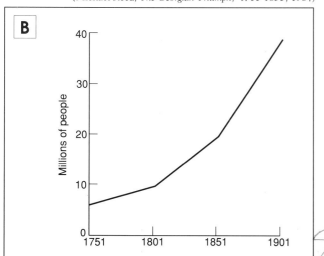

Population growth in Britain, 1751-1901

The rise in population made a huge impact because there had been a big change in where people lived. It wasn't until I picked out key towns and cities for table **G** that I grasped just how quickly towns had grown. By 1851 there were more people living in towns than in the country, **D**. Population increase meant that there were lots of workers ready to work for very low wages in the new factories, in the mines, on the roads and railways, and lots of people to buy what was made.

The rapid growth of both old and new towns was to cause huge problems for health, housing, religion, education and looking after the old, the ill and the out-of-work. People flooded in from the countryside to the towns, and were often on the move seeking work. I came across the rather haunting folk-song, **F**, which shows what this might have meant.

 *It's hard when folks can't find th' work*
Weer they've been bred and born;
When I were young I allus thowt
I'd bide 'midst royits and corn.
But I've been forced to work in t' towns
So here's my litany:
From Hull and Halifax and Hell,
Good Lord deliver me.

When I were courting Mary Jane,
T' old squire he says, one day,
'I've got na bield for wedded folk,
Choose will ta wed or stay.'
I could na give up t' lass I loved,
So to t' town we 'ad to flee:
From Hull and Halifax and Hell,
Good Lord deliver me.

I've walked at neet through Sheffield loyns -
Twere same as being i' hell -
Where furnaces thrust out tongues of fire
And reared like t' wind on t' fell.
I've sammed up coils i' Barnsley pits
Wi' muck up to my knee:
From Sheffield, Barnsley, Rotherham,
Good Lord deliver me.

I've seen fog creep across Leeds brig
As thick as Bastille soup.
I've lived weer folks were stowed away
Like rabbits in a coop. **(F)**

(Anon., *The Dalesman's Litany*)

FACTFILE

E

Reasons for falling death-rate and rising birth-rate

People married earlier and had more children.

Changes in agriculture (the Agricultural Revolution) meant more and better food. Fresh meat and vegetables produced a more varied diet.

Industrial growth helped people become healthier - new brick houses, cheap cotton clothing and soap all helped.

Towns became healthier after 1800 with the building of sewers, the piping of fresh water and the paving of streets.

The Government passed Acts in 1848 and 1875 which helped improve public health.

Inoculation cut the number of deaths from smallpox.

Medical care became much better. Fewer women and babies died in childbirth.

G	Population in '000s				
	pre 1801	1801	1821	1841	1861
London	775	959	1139	1948	2804
Birmingham	42	71	102	183	296
Bolton	12	18	32	51	70
Bradford	4	13	26	67	106
Brighton	3	7	24	47	78
Coventry	15	16	21	31	41
Liverpool	35	82	138	286	444
Shrewsbury	11	15	20	18	22

(Source: Eric Evans, *The Forging of the Modern State*, 1983, adapted)

One result of the growing population was an increase in emigration from Britain to America, Canada or Australia, **H**. I was staggered when I looked at these figures and compared them with the total number of people living in Britain. Can you guess why I was so surprised?

H	Emigration in '000s			
	USA	**Canada**	**Australia**	**Total**
1855	86	16	47	150
1860	68	3	21	96
1865	118	14	37	175
1870	153	27	17	203
1875	81	12	35	141
1880	167	21	24	228
1885	138	20	39	208
1890	152	23	21	218
1895	127	17	11	185
1900	103	18	15	169
TOTALS	**1193**	**171**	**267**	**1773**

(Source: B.R. Mitchell, *Abstract of British Historical Statistics*, 1971)

In 1798 population growth led to a huge public scare. In a famous book, Thomas Malthus argued that population grew geometrically. Malthus said that a couple could have four children, their four children could marry and produce 16 grandchildren, the 16 grandchildren could have 64 children and so on.

The problem was that the amount of food we could grow was limited because we would run out of land. Can you think what Malthus claimed would be the long term result of a geometric growth in population? The ideas of Malthus were to have a profound impact on how the ruling classes treated poor people for the next 100 years. Can you think why, and how?

Population Explosion!

A children's magazine is holding a contest for a history wallchart. Its theme is how population growth harms the environment.

You have to prepare such a wallchart on your own, in pairs or in groups.

The class can split into seven groups, with each group preparing its ideas on one of the topics below.

Then form **new groups,** with no more than one or two from each of the seven original groups in any one of the new groups. Each new group then makes its own chart, which pools ideas and information.

1 Researching topics (AT3)
• **Britain before population growth** - what it was like both in towns and in the countryside.
• **The population growth** - possible reasons for this.
• **The growth of towns** - what towns were like due to growing population.
• **Emigration** - how and why people left Britain to live abroad.
• **Folk-songs on population growth** - work out what **F** means and put it into modern English. Make up your own folk-song and either recite it or sing it.
• **Malthus** - the growth of population, ideas about him.
• **Figures** - graphs, maps and tables showing growth.

2 Preparing the chart (AT2, AT1)
• Think of a heading for your chart.
• Take each topic and work out how you are going to present it on the chart.
• Work out how the chart should look - each group member can do this and then everyone should agree on one idea.
• Present your finished chart. The class can hold a chart-judging contest, with the best chart winning.

ACTIVITY · ACTIVITY ·

The Agricultural Revolution

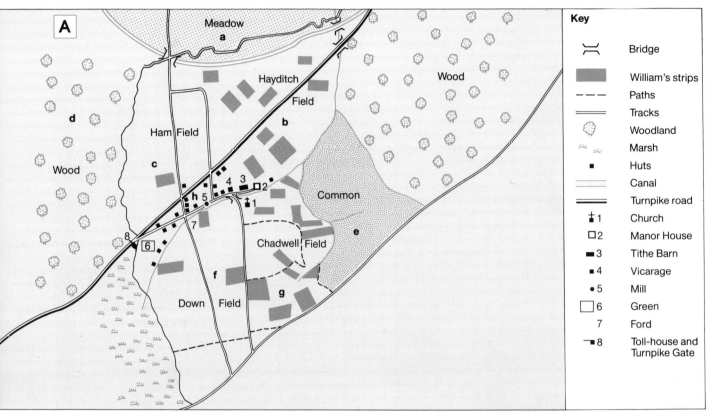

William farmed the land in the old medieval village of Newton

1804. William Hurrell's mind was racing - he had been to a meeting with **Arthur Young**, the famous writer on changes in farming. They had talked for hours about the new farming methods. What a lot to think about! Arthur had argued that it was only through thousands of landlords like William **changing** their ways of farming that an agricultural revolution would happen. The high price of food would pay William to alter the way he ran his 400-acre farm in Newton, **A**. Wheat and meat had soared in price from 1790 to 1804, and costs and wages had not kept pace. New farming methods and new crops would mean a big increase in the yield of crops and in the number, size and quality of the animals reared.

Newton was an open-field village with four open fields, a common and woodland. In other parts of England most of the land had been fenced in or enclosed in the past, **B**. At Newton, William still farmed in the medieval way, rotating his crops (see pages 62-63 in *Medieval Realms*). Arthur Young had given William a copy of his book on new farming methods in Norfolk. In factfile **C** I have sorted out the main ideas and methods that William would have heard about for improving the land and crops on his farm. I based **C** on a university book about the Agricultural Revolution.

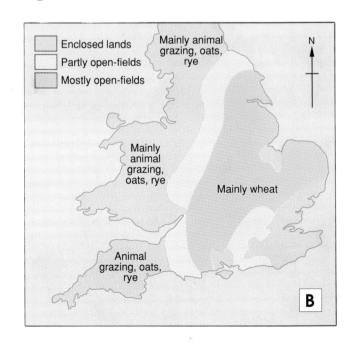

C

NEW CROPS

Turnips Although common, they would not last through a severe winter and did not do the land as much good as grasses.

Swedes A newer root crop which seemed to be better for the soil than turnips.

Clover/lucerne (grass) Clover was an excellent crop to enrich the soil with nitrogen. Lucerne - a better kind of grass - was used to make hay to feed the animals in winter.

IMPROVED SOIL

Marling Spreading chalk on the land at £2.00 an acre made it much more fertile.

Manuring Keeping a large flock of sheep - whose main job was dropping their manure on the land - made the land richer.

Draining Draining the land at £1.50 an acre meant much heavier crops of wheat and barley than before, and more grass and hay.

ANIMALS

Sheep Bakewell's Leicester breed - their meat was very fatty and did not sell well, and their wool was nothing special. (Bakewell was Britain's most famous animal improver.) **Or** Ellman's new Southdowns - they had good meat and wool. (William would need a flock of 500 for his Newton farm.)

Horses Bakewell had helped breed a new kind of large shire-horse. (William would need 24 at £30 each.)

Cattle Improved Shorthorns were a new breed that gave more meat and more milk. (200 would be plenty for William.)

NEW AND BETTER MACHINES

The Rotherham plough, rollers and harrows Ransomes of Ipswich made a new, smaller and lighter plough - with a cast-iron plough share which needed fewer horses or oxen to pull it. You could also buy spare parts for it! Ransomes also sold heavy rollers and harrows made out of iron. (Vital to help break up William's heavy soil.)

Seed drills Only a few farmers used seed drills which Jethro Tull had made famous 70 years before.

Threshing machine This would be quicker than using flails to thresh the corn.

NEW BUILDINGS

A new farm (William could build a brand new farm in Down Field to replace the old one in the village. The farm would contain all the features in **D**.)

A new threshing shed

A new barn for hay and straw.

D

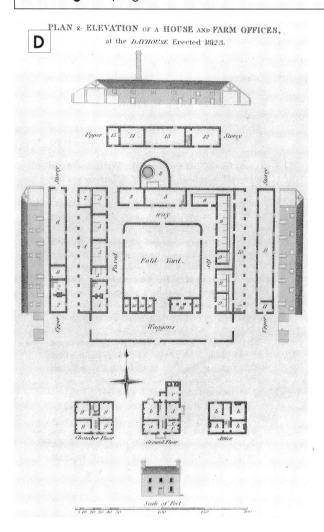

PLAN & ELEVATION OF A HOUSE AND FARM OFFICES, at the DAYHOUSE Erected 1823.

Farm Catalogue

William would have talked about changes with his farm manager. William's land was low lying, with a heavy, clay soil. The strips were scattered around the four fields. You and William have to choose up to **two** ideas from each of the five main headings in **C.**

1 Researching (AT3)
You walk around the village fields - what might you see at **a-e**? Think about each of the points in **C**, and what use they might be to William. Find out about changes in farming before 1804.

2 Decision (AT1)
On your own or in pairs, decide which things you would choose from **C**.

3 Farm advice (AT1)
Make out a list of your plans for the farm. What do you think the consequences of your decisions might be?

11

Enclosure

1806. How was William Hurrell going to make more money out of his 400 acres in Newton? The answer seemed to be **enclosure** - the fencing in of the open fields and sharing out of the village's land among the landowners. Already thousands of villages had had their lands enclosed. Farmers could make much more money from enclosed land than they could from their strips in the open fields. **Points 1-5** below suggest why - I took them from a number of history books on enclosure.

1 Wasted time Strips spread out among the common fields meant that William's farm workers wasted a huge amount of time walking from strip to strip.

2 Unfarmed land (fallow) With the old crop-rotation system, every four years one of the fields was left fallow or unworked. This was to allow animals to graze on the field so that their manure would enrich the soil.

3 Extra land The common would now be shared out among the farmers, giving them more land for themselves.

4 Control of disease No longer would disease spread like wildfire among the sheep, cows and horses kept on the common or in the open fields, as source **A** suggested to me. Disease among

crops was also easier to keep in check.

5 Farm planning William could now plan how he would run his farm without having to take into account what the other villagers wanted to do. He could grow any new crops he wanted, and breed his cows, sheep and horses along the latest lines.

William was sure that he would get the backing of the biggest landowner in Newton, Richard Bendysh, who owned 800 acres. Between them Richard and William owned 60% of the village - but after 1801 a village needed owners of 80% of the land to get an Act of Parliament passed to enclose its lands.

In 1806 Richard and William made their first move to enclose Newton and called a public meeting in the local pub to talk about it. At the meeting they had to listen to points for and against enclosure, but they had already made up their minds to press on with their enclosure plans. By 1810, under an Enclosure Act, three commissioners had shared out the land of the village and the village had been enclosed. Before this the commissioners had visited Waltham, in Lincolnshire, **B** and **C**, to get some ideas to help them share out the land.

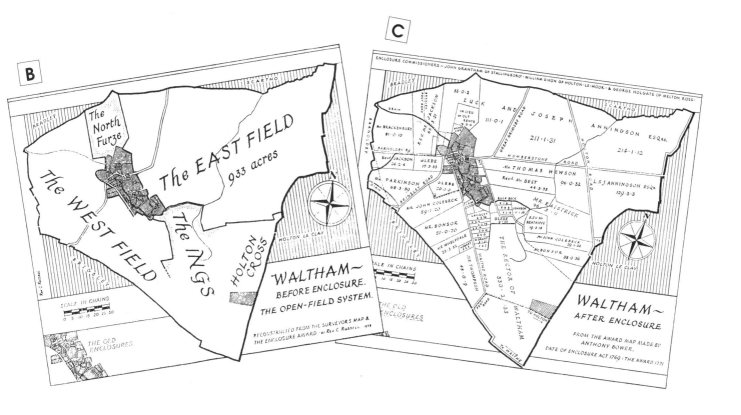

B — WALTHAM ~ BEFORE ENCLOSURE. THE OPEN-FIELD SYSTEM.

C — WALTHAM ~ AFTER ENCLOSURE

Enclosure!

You can plan a drama or re-enactment of how the enclosure of Newton might have gone. Work through the scenes by yourself, or split up the scenes among groups in the class, with each group taking part in a different scene.

1 The village meeting (AT2)

Present will be William Hurrell (400 acres), Richard Bendysh (800 acres), two yeoman families and the vicar with 50 acre strips each, six families with 25 strips each, seven families with 10 strips each, 14 families with a double strip and five squatter families who have no land and live in hovels on the common.
Enclosure will cost £2.00 a strip, and only those with 25 strips or more can afford it.

2 The debate (AT2)

William's agent, John Ashby (the teacher), will control the debate. Each of you can take the role of one family. In turn, each family can say what it thinks about enclosure, and answer questions from other families about its thoughts and feelings. A vote will be taken to see if the village is in favour of enclosure - by adding up the amount of land in favour of enclosure. If it is four-fifths of the total, the village will be enclosed.

3 The enclosure (AT2, AT3)

On your own or in groups, work out on a large-scale map of Newton how the land might have been split up after an Enclosure Act. The village, with the common, woods, meadow and fields, covers 2000 acres in all. Hurrell and Bendysh will have their land in large blocks. Each will build a new farm in the middle of his land, with a carriage track to the nearest road. The other landowners' blocks will be in **one** of the fields. Roads and hedges will be straight.

4 The villagers (AT1)

A year after enclosure only 10 farmers are left in the village. The families with fewer than 10 strips have sold their land and now live as farm workers. Each family talks about what has happened to it, and then answers questions from other villagers.

5 Closing speech (AT2)

Write a speech to close the drama from the viewpoint of **either** a member of today's Green Party who backs old ways of living and organic farming **or** a modern farmer who thinks that the only way a farm can survive is if it uses the latest ideas.

ACTIVITY · ACTIVITY

The New Farm

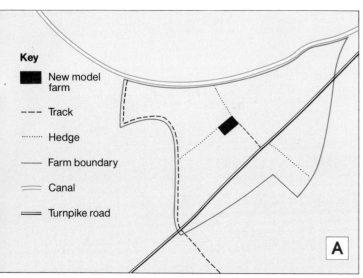

Key
- ⬛ New model farm
- --- Track
- ······ Hedge
- ── Farm boundary
- ═ Canal
- ═ Turnpike road

A

year **crop rotation**, sowing a new crop - turnips, barley, clover or wheat - in each field each year. William and John got their ideas about what to grow in the four fields from Arthur Young's book.

Why do you think this was a better system than medieval crop rotation? **B** gives you a clue, while **C** lists the farm work done during the year.

Wheat	A main grain crop, prices are high. Takes goodness out of the soil.
Barley	A main grain crop with high prices.
Clover/sanfoin [grass]	Clover puts goodness back into the soil. Sheep eat the grass and manure the soil. Hay made from grass to feed animals in winter.
Turnips/swedes/ mangels	Animals eat them in winter. **B**

November. I have just ordered the seeds that I plan to grow in my garden next year. Now I have to work out where, how and when I am going to plant them. In 1814 William Hurrell and John Ashby also had to plan their farm in Newton along new lines, **A**. They decided to have a four-

C Month	Jobs
January	Hedge, ditch, odd jobs, sheep on turnip field.
February	Hedge, ditch, lambing of sheep on turnip field.
March	Plough the stubble of old wheat, plough barley and turnip fields. Harrow the ploughed land ready for sowing. Get weeds and coarse grass out of ground.
April	Sow barley and wheat, with clover and grass seed.
May	Three ploughings and harrowing for turnips, with lime and manure being ploughed in. Mow clover field for hay.
June	Sow turnips.
July	Hoe turnips.
August	Wheat and barley harvest.
September	Thresh the grain. Harrow winter wheat field.
October	Plough, harrow and then sow winter wheat field.
November December }	Plough and harrow field for sowing barley next April. Keep sheep on turnip field.

The Farm Planner

Today working farm museums are very popular. You decide to set up a farm along the lines of William Hurrell's at Newton. Make out a chart for a four-year crop rotation of turnips, barley, clover and wheat.

1 Study the evidence (AT3)
Study **B** and **C**. Decide which crops you would grow in which field, where you would keep your animals and what improvements you would make in each year.

2 Your chart (AT2)
Draw up your chart for four years:

FARM PLANNER .... YEAR			
Field	Crops/Animals	Planting/ Improve- ments	Harvesting

ACTIVITY · ACTIVITY

14

Farming 1850-1900

I chose **A** from a school textbook for 14- to 16-year-olds to show you how to read and make sense of such a source.

❝ *The 'Golden Age' of Farming (1846-1870)*
This period was one of high profits for farmers.

Reasons for the Expansion and Prosperity of Farming from 1846 to 1870

(i) Population
There was an increasing demand for food in Britain. The population increased from 17 million in 1846 to 24 million in 1874.

(ii) Railways
The new railways carried large amounts of meat, milk and vegetables from country areas to towns. They carried fertilisers, cattle-cake and farm machinery from ports and cities to farms.

(iii) Lack of Foreign Competition
Parliament had repealed the Corn Laws in 1846 but foreign grain did not swamp the market as some MPs had predicted.

(iv) Education
Farmers could also learn about the latest farming techniques by reading the journals of the Royal Agricultural Society and by attending agricultural shows.

(v) Technical Improvements
All the time, thousands of improvements were being made to farming methods, crops and animals.

Drainage
John Fowler devised a drainage plough (or 'mole plough') which could lay clay pipes for 5 shillings (25p) an acre.

Fertilisers
In 1843, Sir John Lawes started to manufacture superphosphates at his factory in Deptford. At the same time guano (seagull droppings rich in chemicals) were being sent to Britain from Peru. Nitrates were sent from Chile and potash from Germany.

New machines
An improved version of Tull's seed drill became popular with farmers. A reliable reaping machine was produced in the USA by McCormick and introduced into Britain in the 1850s.

(vi) Livestock
There was considerable interest in pedigree cattle breeding using Bakewell's methods.

(vii) Wages
During this period the wages for farm workers remained low. Farmers could therefore keep their labour costs down.

The Great Depression (1870-1914)
There was a sudden depression in farming after 1870 which resulted in many changes in agriculture. Between 1873 and 1879 there was a series of wet summers and poor harvests. ❞ **(A)**

(Simon Mason, *Work Out Social and Economic History GCSE*)

Radio Report

1 Reading history (AT1, AT3)
To 'think history' you need to be able to sort out information and ideas from a secondary source like **A**. You can use the points below to help you or you can follow your own plan:

• We start with **key questions**. Mine is: **What caused the 'Golden Age' of Farming?** Jot down any other questions you could ask.
• **Quick reading**. Skim read **A**, making a list of words or phrases that are not clear. Use a dictionary to work out their meaning.
• Read the piece quickly again, noting all the facts you can find.
• Jot down the writer's main points.
• Discuss them with your partner or as a class.
• **Slow reading.** Read the passage slowly. List the **key words** and **sentences**.
• **Draw** a star diagram for the question: What caused the 'Golden Age' of Farming?
• **Check** to see which points in your diagram are the same or different from your partner's.
• As a class, **work out** a star diagram for the question.
• **Research** in other books to find out more about the points you have worked out.
• **Reporting.** Produce a **thirty-second** report for a radio news programme on British farming from 1850 to 1870. In it put forward what you think caused the 'Golden Age' of Farming.

ACTIVITY ACTIVITY

The Transport Revolution

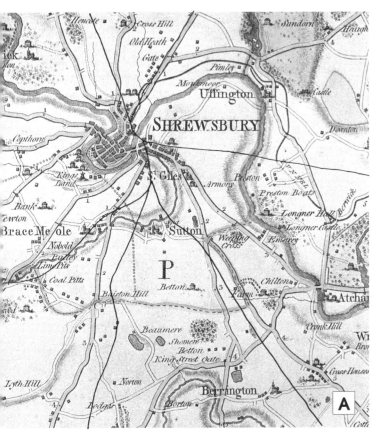

List the ways in which you can travel to school, to the shops in your nearest town, to the seaside or to London and to a holiday abroad. Then try and think how you would have made the same trips in 1750, 1820 and 1900. I chose map **A** of the area where I used to live because it is packed with clues to help you answer these questions. In your local library or record office there will be similar maps of the area around your school.

Before 1750 Celia Fiennes went from Exeter, my present home, to Plymouth. For the last 24 miles:

... the roades contracts and the lanes are exceeding [very] narrow and so cover'd up you can see little about. An army might be marching undiscovered by any body, for when you are on those heights that shews a vast country about, you cannot see one road. The wayes now became so difficult that one could scarcely pass by each other, even the single horses, and so dirty in many places and just a track for one horses feete, and the banks on either side so neer. **(B)**

In summer, tracks became dust bowls, in winter they were mud baths. There are even stories of travellers drowning in huge potholes in roads. Each parish was supposed to mend its own roads, but there was little work done to keep the roads in good shape.

History forces you to think yourself back into the past to try and see why and how things **changed.** From 1700 **changes** began in how people could travel. The changes made journeys quicker, easier and cheaper. Between 1700 and 1800, turnpike trusts built over 20,000 miles of new roads, see pages 18-19, along which carts and stage-coaches could pass with ease, as **C** suggests. In the 1760s a revolution in water transport began. By 1820 a spider's web of canals covered the whole country, see pages 22-23. The final change was the coming of the railways. Between 1830 and 1880 a network of railways developed which reached every corner of the British Isles, see pages 26-27. London was less than a day's travel from anywhere in England - before 1800 the trip could have taken weeks. **D** is my favourite early railway picture.

History of Transport Guide

You have to prepare a one-sheet guide on the history of transport for tourists to show the main changes in transport from 1750 to 1900. Base your guide on an outline of map **A** or on a similar map of your own area. You can split up the work among you. **Or** you can design a Christmas card using pictures **C** and **D** to give an idea of how transport changed from about 1750 to 1850.

1 Working on your sources (AT3)
• Trace the outline of map **A**. Mark on it the main rivers and the towns and villages.
• Put a key on your map for the following:
1750 Old roads and tracks (all roads).
1750-1800 Turnpikes (roads with a thick line on one side). How many milestones and turnpike gates can you spot?
1790-1830 Canals (thick grey line from Shrewsbury).
1830-1880 Railways (three thin lines).
• Suggest where visitors might go to see **evidence** of early turnpike roads, canals and railways.
• Read **B** quickly. Put down the thoughts you have of road travel before 1750. Go through **B** slowly and work out what all the words and phrases mean. Then add new ideas to your

thoughts by imagining what travel might have been like: on a hot summer's day; in a gale; in a snowstorm; after it had been raining for a week.

2 Timetable (AT1, AT3)
Make out a table showing how you would have sent a 20-tonne load of limestone from Brace Meole to Berwick in 1750, 1800, 1850 and today. Using the facts below, work out how long it would have taken you in each case.

Name	Load	Speed	Workmen
Packhorse	100 kg	2 mph	1
Wagon	2 tonnes	2 mph	1
Barge	10 tonnes	2 mph	1
Train	20 tonnes	30 mph	1
Lorry	20 tonnes	30 mph	1

Your table headings are:
Date From To Method No. of workmen Time

3 Notes (AT1)
Write a caption and three lines of notes about what your trip might have been like in **C** in 1750, and in **D** in 1830. Use **C** and **D** in your tourist guide, and include anything else you can find out about travel around these dates.

ACTIVITY · ACTIVITY ·

Roads

A TABLE of the TOLLS payable at this TURNPIKE GATE.
[By the Local Act.]

	s d
FOR every Horse, Mule, Afs, or other Beast (Except Dogs) drawing any Coach, Berlin, Landau, Barouche, Chariot, Chaise, Chair, Hearse, Gig, Curricle, Whiskey, Taxed Cart, Waggon, Wain, Timber frame, Cart frame Dray or other Vehicle of whatsoever description when drawn by more than one Horse or other Beast the Sum of Four pence half-penny Such Waggon, Wain, Cart, or other such Carriage having Wheels of lefs breadth than four and a half inches	" 4½
AND when drawn by one Horse or other Beast only the sum of six-pence (Waggons, Wains and other such Carriages having Wheels as aforesaid)	" 6
FOR every Dog drawing any Truck, Barrow or other Carriage for the space of One Hundred Yards or upwards upon any part of the said Roads, the Sum of One Penny	" 1
FOR every Horse, Mule, Afs, or other Beast laden or unladen and not drawing, the Sum of Two-pence	" 2
FOR every carriage moved or propelled by Steam or Machinery or by any other power than Animal power the Sum of one Shilling for each Wheel thereof	1 0
FOR every Score of Oxen, Cows or neat Cattle, the Sum of Ten-pence and so in Proportion for any greater or lefs Number	" 10
FOR every Score of Calves, Sheep, Lambs or Swine the Sum of Five pence and so in proportion for any greater or lefs Number	" 5
(By 4. G. 4. C. 95)	
FOR every Horse, Mule, Afs or other Beast drawing any Waggon Wain, Cart or other such Carriage having the Fellies of the Wheels of the breadth of Six Inches or upwards at the Bottom when drawn by more than one Horse, Mule, Afs or other Beast the Sum of Three-pence	" 3
AND when drawn by one Horse, Mule, Afs or other Beast the Sum of Four-Pence (Except Carts)	" 4
FOR every Horse, Mule, Afs or other Beast drawing any Waggon Wain, Cart or other such Carriage having the Fellies of the Wheels of the Breadth of four inches and a half and lefs than Six inches when drawn by more than one Horse, Mule, Afs or other Beast the Sum of Three-pence three farthings	" 3¾
AND when drawn by one Horse, Mule, Afs or other Beast the Sum of Five-pence (Except Carts)	" 5
FOR every Horse, Mule, Afs or other Beast drawing any Cart with Wheels of every Breadth when drawn by only one such Animal the Sum of Six Pence	" 6

NB Two Oxen or neat Cattle drawing shall be considered as one Horse
3. G. 4. C. 126.

CARRIAGES with four Wheels affixed to any Waggon or Cart
all as if drawn by two Horses. Carriages with two Wheels so
d pay Toll as if drawn by one Horse but such Carriages are
Tolls if conveying any Goods other than
for Protection.

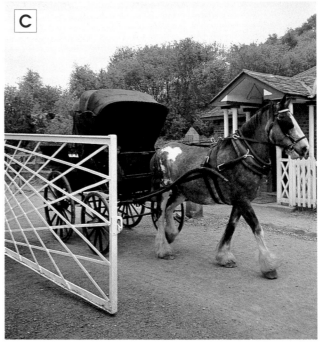

How can you make sense of the huge changes that took place in road building from around 1700 to 1830?

The first thing to grasp is that in each area the local landowners, merchants, industrialists and traders would have set up firms or companies to build new roads. These firms were called 'turnpike trusts'.

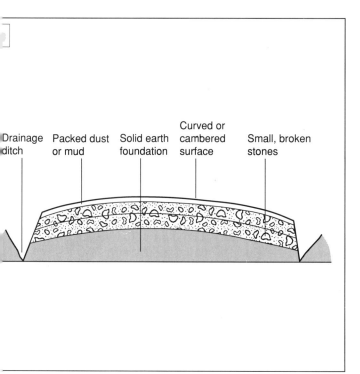

Cross-section of a Macadam road

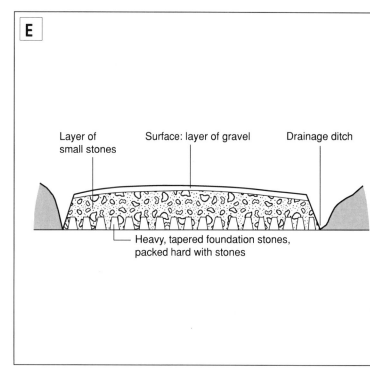

Cross-section of a Telford road

To build its roads, a turnpike trust would raise money mainly from local banks, farmers, landlords and traders. The turnpike was the gate where you had to pay money, a toll, to use the road, **C**. A toll-board would tell you how much you had to pay, **A**. The trust would use the tolls to run the road and to pay back the money spent on building it. Any cash left was profit.

Turnpike trusts have left behind clues, such as toll-houses where the tolls were collected and milestones, **B**. Keep a look-out for them next time you go for a long car or bus ride.

Turnpike trusts spread like wildfire and their new roads formed a network which linked up the towns and villages of Britain. The trusts would pay road builders to plan and build their roads with bridges, toll-houses, turnpike gates and cuttings. The most famous road builders were Macadam and Thomas Telford. Macadam built a cheap road that rested on a dry base. The surface was made up of tiny stones, chippings and earth which packed down firmly, **D**. Telford's roads cost a lot more but had a much better base or foundation, **E**.

Turnpike Company!

You can create and play a turnpike game using your local ordnance survey map **(AT1, AT3)**.

• Take an A4 page of the map and trace over all the A-roads and B-roads on it and the **towns** or **town centres**.
• Two or more can play. Each of you chooses a town which is 10 kilometres or more from the next person's town.
• In each round you build five kilometres of road which you mark on the map. You build your road along the routes of A-roads or B-roads. Your road

cannot **cross** or **go along** the roads of another turnpike. After your turn the next player puts in his or her road. Take turns in alphabetical order of surnames. A round represents one year.
• For each five kilometres of A-road, you get £100 income a year; for every five kilometres of B-road, you get £50 income.
• Work out how you will plan your road network, and keep a score of how much money you make. The game ends after an agreed number of rounds or when you can build no more road. The winner is the one with the highest income per year!

ACTIVITY · ACTIVITY ·

Turnpike!

I always use map **A** to show how a turnpike road was built. The map highlights the problems that faced road builders like Telford, and is based on roads he built near to where I used to live.

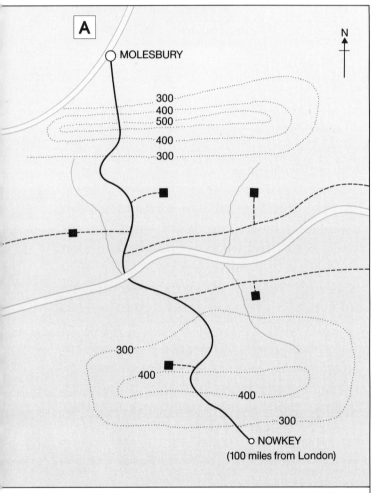

A

MOLESBURY

300
400
500
400
300

300
400
400
300

NOWKEY
(100 miles from London)

1 mile

Key

⊔ Bridge (large)

⇊ Bridge

▪ Milestone

╬□ Toll-house and turnpike gate

C ■ Coaching inn

■ Squire's houses

····500···· Contour

------- Track

——— Old track

〜〜 Stream

River

The Impact of Roads

Turnpike roads made it much easier to bring fresh food to market and carry heavy loads. In every area hundreds of carriers used their wagons to carry light and heavy goods, such as cotton clothes, pots, pans, cups, coal and clay, to and from mines and factories and to markets, shops and warehouses.

A	The impact of roads on travel times		
LONDON to	1750	1770	1830
Bristol	3 days	2 days	1 day
Edinburgh	12 days	4 days	3 days
Exeter	4 days	2 days	1 day
Newcastle	6 days	3 days	2 days

What does the design of this vehicle suggest about the influence of new roads?

66 *That the carrier network was reliable and efficient is clear from the business records of Abraham Dent, shopkeeper, of Kirby Stephen. In his shop he and his father sold tea, sugar, flour, braid, magazines, gunpowder and patent medicine. He drew his goods from suppliers in Kendal, Cockermouth, Liverpool, Manchester, Barnard Castle, Newcastle and London. The journey to London took about a fortnight, but goods rarely went astray.* 99 **(C)**

(Michael Reed, *The Georgian Triumph, 1700-1830*, 1984)

66 *The roads of West Devonshire are, at present, most remarkable for their steepness. Less than half a century ago, they were mere gullies, worn by torrents in the rocks ... At length, however, good turnpike roads were formed, between town and town, throughout this quarter of the Island; and most of the villages have carriage roads opened to them.* 99 **(D)**

(W. G. Hoskins, *Devon and its People*, 1959)

The Talk

You have to prepare a talk for eight-year-olds on the impact of turnpike roads. Use pictures to help. You have a pile of cuttings from old books, **A-D**.

1 Research (AT1, AT3)
Decide which topics you will cover and sort out the facts and pictures you want to include. Find out anything else you can, using books, magazines and any other sources.

2 Presentation (AT2, AT1)
How will you present your ideas? You might take a point of view - you could be a member of the Green Party or a backer of the motor car. Think about using some of these: a large-scale map; a xerox of a mail-coach with labels; a competition to plan a cart; a poem about riding on a mail-coach; a talk between an old coachman and a schoolchild about how road travel has changed in the last 50 years; a display of pictures or adverts for mail-coaches and carriers' carts.

ACTIVITY · ACTIVITY

The Canal Age

Weddings are wonderful. I have just been to one where, while waiting for the bride to turn up, I leafed through a book on the history of the Llangollen Canal. Suddenly I began to see how canals had been at the heart of the working life of a region. The canal had acted as a huge reservoir. Water from it had turned the grindstones of corn mills, worked the machines in factories and sawmills and driven pumps to drain marshes. Along the canal had come coal, clay, raw materials, lime and sand. Farmers had used the lime and sand to enrich heavy, clay soil. The canal had carried grain, cattle, vegetables and locally made goods back to the towns and cities. Canals had been the motorways of their day. They had made sure that there was a **mass market** for the **food** that the Agricultural Revolution grew and for the **products** made in the Industrial Revolution's factories.

How and why did the **Canal Age** start? The idea of canals didn't spring out of fresh air. For hundreds of years there had been massive work done on Britain's rivers. The sea and rivers were the only way of carrying heavy goods over long distances - can you think why? Dams, dykes and cuttings meant that many rivers were almost canals - the only things missing were **locks**.

In Lancashire, in 1755, the first attempt was made to turn a river into a canal when the Sankey Cut was built along the bed of the Sankey Brook, **A**. In 1761 James Brindley built the first real canal for the Duke of Bridgewater. It linked his coal mines at Worsley to Manchester, 10 miles away. Brindley's canal is famous for having the first aqueduct to be built in Britain since Roman times. **B** is the best early picture I could find of it.

Behind the idea of canals was the wish to make money - the canal slashed the cost of sending

Map A

A

Worsley Canal – connected the Duke's Worsley coal-mines with Manchester

R. Irwell

Worsley

Manchester

Aqueduct over *R. Irwell* — Irwell

R. Mersey

R. Mersey

St. Helens

Warrington

Liverpool

Widnes

Runcorn

Bridgewater Canal – (1762-67)

Northwich

CHESHIRE SALT FIELD

Sankey Brook Canal (1755) – connected the coal-mines at St. Helens with Liverpool and the Cheshire salt-mines

Grand Trunk Canal (1766-1777) – connected the *Trent* and the *Mersey*, linking the *North* and *Irish seas*

R. Weaver

R. Trent

THE POTTERIES

What do you think is being carried in the barge? How is the barge powered? Where might it have come from, and where is it going?

coal from Worsley to Manchester. Profits soared as the cost of buying coal fell by half. What might this do to the cost of making cotton goods, the demand for them and factory owners' profits? Soon a network of canals tied into the network of turnpike roads to link town and country, mines and mills. The same transport pattern grew all over Britain, **C**. From 1789 to 1794

'canal mania' gripped Britain, with the setting up of hundreds of canal companies. If you wanted to build a canal you took the same steps as for building a turnpike, see page 18. The Canal Age lasted from 1760 to 1830. It left behind hundreds of miles of canals. Around 1830 a new, quicker and cheaper form of travel took over. Can you guess what it was?

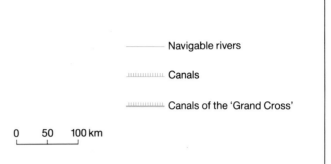

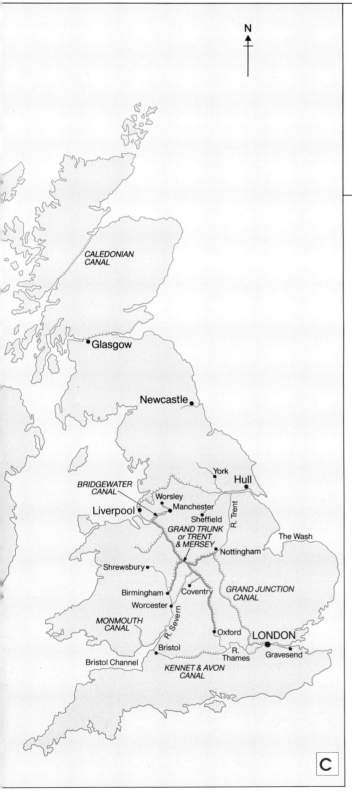

Canals and navigable rivers, c.1800

Information Book

You have to prepare two double-page spreads for an information book on the history of canals. Work on your own or with a friend.

1 Choosing and researching your spreads (AT1, AT3)
- One spread will be on the growth of canals, the other on anything about canals that interests you.
- Each spread is two pages. On the left page there should be text of about 90 words; on the right page, a picture that ties into your text.
- Sort out the facts and ideas you want to include and find out about them.

2 Drafting and drawing (AT2, AT1)
- Decide on the point of view you want to take in your spreads.
- Give each spread a title.
- Draw up a draft of the two 90-word texts.
- When you are sure they are both in the form you want, write them out neatly.
- Do a rough plan for your two drawings, with labels for each.
- Then do a neat copy of each one and include its title.

3 Your canal book (AT1)
Choose the best spreads to make a class canal book.

Canal Mania

You can create and play a game which will help you get an idea of what 'canal mania' was like from 1789 to 1794.

a **The game** is for two sets of teams - **one** set represents four or five canal companies, the **other** represents rich people buying shares in the companies. The class splits into **groups** of **three or four** players. Each group will represent a canal company.

b You will belong to **both** sets of players. The game will be played **twice**, once with you as a **canal company**, the second time with you as a **person** buying shares in canal companies.

c **Canal company**. A canal is planned between Molesbury and Nowkey, see page 20. You decide to set up a company to compete for the route. You belong to a team of **three or four players**. You have to prepare a **plan** for your canal route and sell **shares** in it to rich people in the region - people like bankers, farmers, gentry, doctors, mill-owners and merchants.

d **Each canal company** has to produce the following things in order to try and sell shares to the public:
- A **sales poster** advertising the canal.
- An **account** of the benefits the canal will bring to the region (maximum 200 words).
- Share certificates. **Prepare 30 share certificates** for sale to the public.
- An **account** of what the canal will cost to build after you have made the **plan**.
- A **plan** of the route with the following on it:

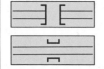

A tunnel - cost: £1000 per one-tenth of a mile

An aqueduct - to carry the canal across a stream or river. Cost: £1000

Bridges - where a road crosses the canal, a bridge will cost £500; for a track, the bridge will cost £100

Wharves - these will be built for loading and unloading where the canal crosses a turnpike

road. They will also be built at either end of the canal. Cost: £100 each

Warehouse - at each wharf there will be a warehouse. Cost: £100

Locks - these will be needed where the canal has to rise 10 feet. Cost of each lock: £200

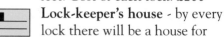

Lock-keeper's house - by every lock there will be a house for the lock-keeper. He takes tolls from the bargees for using the lock. Cost: £50

Basins - canal basins will be built near the lock-keeper's house. Cost: £100 each

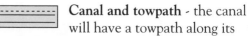

Canal and towpath - the canal will have a towpath along its side for the horses who pull the barges. Canal and towpath will cost £1000 per mile.

e **Shareholders**. When you have prepared your canal company plan you then become a rich person who wants to buy shares. Each of you has to prepare **10** bank notes to add up to £1000. **The teacher collects these in**. The notes can be used to buy shares in **canal companies**.

f **The contest**
- For each contest the class splits into **two** teams - one representing canal companies, the other shareholders.
- **Four or five** canal companies will present their plans for their canals, and then they will try and **sell** shares to the rich people.
- The teacher hands out £1500 of banknotes to each rich person.
- The contest ends after a set period of trading.
- **The winning company** - the one that will **win the contract** to build the canal - is the one that has raised the **most money** from selling shares.

g For the **second game**, the **shareholders** become **canal companies** and the **canal companies** become **shareholders**. Follow the same steps as in **f**.

ACTIVITY · ACTIVITY ·

The Impact of Canals

> Monday, 11 September, Malmesbury (Wilts). I saw in one single farmyard here more food than enough for four times the inhabitants of the parish; and this yard did not contain a tenth, perhaps, of the produce of the parish; but, while the poor creatures that raise the wheat and the barley and cheese and the mutton and the beef are living upon potatoes, an accursed Canal comes kindly through the parish to convey away the wheat and all the good food to the tax-eaters and their attendants in the WEN [London]. **(A)**

(William Cobbett, *Rural Rides*, 1830)

> **Coalport** takes its name from the termination [end] of the Shropshire Canal, which is seven miles in length. The coals brought by this conveyance, from the extensive mines of Ketley, Dawley and other places, are landed on the banks of the River Severn, and are thence transported in barges to different parts of the counties of Worcester and Gloucester, to the average amount of fifty thousand tons annually. **(B)**

(T.Gregory, *The Shropshire Gazetteer*, 1824)

A-C are some sources I found to give you a brief idea of the impact that canals had.

The Impact of Canals

This is the title of a British Waterways history competition. You have a single lesson in which to prepare your entry. The **form** it takes is up to you - it can be written, spoken, filmed, drawn, painted, audio-taped, or videoed. **But** your entry must draw on the main points made in sources **A-C,** on facts and ideas on pages 22-23 and on anything else you can find out about the impact of canals.

1 Thinking and researching (AT3, AT1)
On your own or in a pair, decide what approach you will take. Think of your point of view - are canals a good or bad thing? - and what you need to know to present your ideas. Then research your topic.

2 Designing and preparing (AT2, AT1)
Work out a rough plan of what you will do, and then design it.

3 Presenting (AT1)
Present your ideas to the rest of the class, **either** as part of a class wall display where you can all judge what is on show **or** as a talk in front of the class.

ACTIVITY · ACTIVITY

Stourport, a new town, grew up where the Staffordshire and Worcestershire Canal joined the river Severn. Work out the impact the coming of the canals had on the area shown in **C** - it would have been a river with countryside all around it before. Look at **a-e** for clues.

Railways 1800-1830

Think about how you would get to school or go on holiday or on a school trip if cars or coaches were banned. In the age of turnpikes and canals the fastest journeys were at the speed of a trotting horse. From 1800 to 1830 a **change** in travel took place which was to transform how we all live, work and play. **1808, 1814** and **1825** are key dates in the history of the train. I chose sources **A-C** and sorted out factfile **D** to give you some clues about the coming of the railways. In 1830 we enter the **Railway Age** with the opening of the Liverpool-Manchester railway. Between 1830 and 1870 a spider's web of railways grew to cover almost every town and village in England and Wales.

> *The amount of merchandise passing between Liverpool and Manchester has been estimated at 1200 tons a day... The trade of Liverpool has doubled every 20 years ... the trade in cotton has doubled every ten years. Second in importance to cotton is coal. The railway will pass through a rich coalfield... Of coke, culm [coal dust], manure, a large tonnage may be expected. And the tolls on cattle, sheep and pigs, the carriage of parcels, the tolls on heavy machinery, are estimated to produce several thousand pounds a year. Besides these sources of income, there is one the committee believe will make a great deal of money - the tolls on passengers.* **(C)**

(Report by Charles Lawrence, Chairman of the proposed Liverpool-Manchester railway, 1826)

The first steam-engine of the Stockton-Darlington railway, a replica train built for the 1925 centenary

Date	Event	Date	Event
1700+	Tram-ways or wagon-ways used in mining areas to carry heavy loads of coal and ore. Horses pulled wagons along tracks.	1821-25	Stockton-Darlington railway planned and built. A railway company, just like a turnpike or canal company, was set up. George Stephenson planned the route and built the trains. The trains pulled coal at half the cost of horses. In 1825 the Stockton-Darlington railway opened. It was the first railway to carry passengers.
1767	First cast-iron rails in use at Coalbrookdale.		
1800	Steam-engines used to haul wagons up slopes.		
1803	Trevithick built a train which ran along tram-ways for nine miles, from Penydaren to Abercynon in South Wales.	1826	Coal and cotton merchants decided to build a railway between Liverpool and Manchester because they were charged too much to send goods along the canals or turnpike roads. George Stephenson built the line across a huge marsh, the Chat Moss, spanned the Sankey River with a 500-feet viaduct and dug a 2200-yard tunnel.
1808	Trevithick's 'Catch Me Who Can' put on display in Euston Square, London.		
1812+	Trains built to pull coal wagons in the coal mines of the north-east. Trains became bigger, stronger and ran on well-built tracks. Eight-mile-long railway built from the mines to the coal ports on the river Wear.	1829	Rainhill trials to choose the locomotive to run on the Liverpool-Manchester railway - Stephenson's 'Rocket' won.
1818	The idea of a railway from Stockton to Darlington to carry coal was put forward. The railway would make three times more money than a turnpike. A canal would cost far too much to build.	1830	Liverpool-Manchester railway opened.

Railway Postcards

You have to design a set of postcards to show how trains changed from 1800 to 1825 or to 1830 (the opening of the Liverpool-Manchester railway), using sources **A-C** and factfile **D**.

1 Thinking about the sources (AT3, AT1)
Work on your own or in pairs. You can pool your answers to work out ideas as a group or as a class.
• For **A** and **B** answer these questions:
What does the picture show?
Which place does it show?
Why are the trains being used in this way?
• Think of the things you could have heard, seen and smelled, and what thoughts you might have had if you had been sitting with the artist when he or she drew the picture or took the photograph.
• What do the pictures show about how trains **changed** between 1808 and 1825?
• How accurate might the pictures be?
• What other questions might you ask about the pictures?

• How might you answer them?

2 Designing the cards (AT2, AT1)
You have to design one, two or three postcards. Each card should have a title, a picture based on **either A or B**, up to three lines saying what the scene is about, what the trains are used for, and how they may have changed from previous models.

3 A document from the time (AT2, AT3)
You can produce your own documents to go on the back of your postcards. What do you think people shown on **A** and **B** might have written to their best friends about the scenes shown? Each entry should be about 10 lines long, and contain at least five things that you can see in each picture. You can have a class reading and a display of your postcards and documents.

ACTIVITY · ACTIVITY

The Impact of Railways

I used to teach in Crediton, a town in Devon. In May 1851 the railway reached the town. So when my class was about to do the history of railways, I looked at what the local newspaper had said at the time. After the first train had steamed into Crediton a huge party had been held at which the railway chairman had spoken:

Fifteen years since when he first came to Crediton he was unable to get from that place to Exeter without hiring a post-chaise, the only public conveyance being a stage wagon. Since then a gradual improvement had taken place, and they had had omnibuses [horse-drawn bus] and coaches, and now they had to hail this day as the opening for public traffic the Exeter and Crediton Railway ... railways were extending and ramifying [spreading] themselves, not only through England, but over the whole of the civilized world, and they could not afford to be content to travel and jog on at a rate of six miles an hour in a post-chaise, and at a great expense, when all the world was going at four or five times the pace, and at a diminishing [falling] price.

Mr Buller [a local landowner] He recollected the time when they thought it would be a great thing for Crediton if they could have had canal communication [link], and when that idea was abandoned it was hoped they might have had a tram-road. **(A)**

(Exeter Flying Post, 15 May 1851)

B

Lines built by 1836
65 miles built

Lines built by 1850
7,000 miles built

Lines built by 1900
14,000 miles built

Edinburgh
Glasgow
Newcastle
Carlisle
Oldham
Manchester
Hull
Liverpool
Rotherham
Sheffield
Shrewsbury
Birmingham
Merthyr
London
Salisbury
Exeter

What impact did the coming of the railways have? I put in source **B** to give an idea of how lines spread to all parts of Britain and opened them up to trade and travel, and advert **C** to back up this point. Eric Evans, a famous history professor, sums up what the railways meant to Britain:

> Railways were the biggest business Britain had yet seen. Almost a quarter of the expansion [growth] of British national income between 1840 and 1865 was attributable [put down] to railway development. It created new towns, like Crewe, Wolverton, Swindon and Ashford, where engines and rolling-stock were built, and it made possible the new heavy industry town of Middlesbrough, which grew so fast from almost nothing in 1850. **(D)**

(Eric Evans, *The Forging of the Modern State*, 1983)

All kinds of firms sprang up to build and look after trains, carriages, signals and the track - brainstorm what goes in to building and running a railway. Gangs of navvies slaved away to build railways and an army of railway workers ran them, see **E**.

E	The Railway Industry 1847-1860			
	No. of navvies	Miles open	No. of railway workers	Money from goods/passengers
1847	250,000	3,500	45,000	£ 8 million
1850	60,000	6,300	60,000	£13 million
1855	40,000	8,100	100,000	£21 million
1860	55,000	10,200	125,000	£28 million

Railways - Read All About It!

You can create headlines, stories and adverts for a children's history magazine. Your magazine can be about your own area, based on what happened in Crediton. Below are some ideas but you can add your own, using anything else you can find out. Work on your own, in pairs, in groups or as a whole class.

1 Topics (AT3, AT1)
Choose and research **one or more** of these topics and add others:
• The planning and building of the line, and the way it changed the landscape.
• The first train to London; a trip to the seaside; a football special; a day ticket for your area in 1900; an outing to a local city for Christmas shopping; a holiday to Blackpool; emigration to Australia.
• A list of the goods shown in **C**.
• A visit to an engine works and a new railway town.
• A meeting with: a navvy; a local stage-coach owner; a farmer selling cattle and grain; a coal merchant.
• An editorial in 1830, 1860 and 1900 about the impact of railways.
• Local history: evidence in your local area of the railway age. Clues are: bridges, rail track or route, station, hotels, houses, local firms.

2 The story or advert (AT2, AT1)
For each story put: the earliest date that the event could have happened; the title; the first few lines. For your advert make sure you have the date; the goods; where the goods are from; who might buy them; their cost. Do your work in rough and then do a neat copy.

3 Railway collage (AT1)
You can put up your stories and adverts as a classroom collage or display.

4 Railway boom (AT1)
Put the following game into your magazine, and change the rules to improve it.
• Put all large towns and cities on an outline map of Britain.
• Up to four people can take part in the game. Take turns in alphabetical order of your surnames.
• Each person chooses a town or city in which to base a railway company - choose from London (two companies), Exeter or Manchester.
• In each round, build one line from a town or city where you already have a line to any other town or city within 60 kilometres.
• You **cannot** build a line across a rival company's line.
• The winner is the company that builds the most railway lines between towns and cities.

Cottage Industry

List your clothes and the materials they are made of. Can you work out how many things you wear were made in factories and how many were made by hand? What raw materials were used to make them? What tools?

Before 1750 nearly all clothes were hand-made, because factories were few and far between. The main British industry was spinning and weaving wool cloth. **A** is my favourite picture of **cottage industry** - the term we use to describe how most goods were made before the **Industrial Revolution**. Picture **B** on page 63 shows women working, but this time in a **factory.** How many changes can you see in what the women are doing?

In Devon, my home county, scenes like **A** would have been common, for Devon was one of Britain's leading cloth-making districts. In 1750 a farm labourer's wife could earn from 6d to 20d (2.5p to 8p) a day spinning wool into yarn - about half her husband's wage as a weaver.

A

How was cloth made? Let us spend a week with John Briggs, a wool merchant:

Monday - buys wool from a Dartmoor farm after it has been sheared from the sheep.

Tuesday - takes the wool to his spinners in South Tawton, a Devon village, where they spin the wool into yarn.

Wednesday - collects the yarn and takes it to a weaver in the small town of Okehampton, and picks up a bale of cloth.

Thursday - returns to Exeter and leaves the bale at his warehouse, where it will be clipped, washed and dyed.

Friday - sells the bales of cloth at Exeter market. The buyer sends these abroad by ship.

Cottage Industry

You can prepare a study chart for 10-year-olds to show what was involved in making wool cloth.

1 Research (AT3)
• Look at picture **A**. Note **three** things you can say about how the people are working, what **two** of the tools are being used for and what it might have been like to work in that room.
• What ideas do you think the artist is trying to get across?
• Write a short story or poem about the scene from the viewpoint of the little boy near the fire. Describe the room; who the people are; what they do; and a visit from John Briggs to bring wool and collect yarn.

• Find out more about **each** of the steps involved in making wool cloth - look in books for pictures and ideas.

2 The study chart (AT1, AT2)
• Put the **title** at the top of the page.
• Make sure you cover each **stage** in the **process.**
• You can **either** draw **or** photocopy pictures and stick them on to your chart.
• Each picture can have notes on it.
• Include your story or poem.
• As a class, display your study charts and decide whose is best.

ACTIVITY · ACTIVITY ·

The Factory System

Today we think nothing of people working in a factory. Two hundred years ago this was a new idea. Adam Smith, see page six, used the example of a pin factory to show what factory work meant:

❝ *One man draws out the wire, another straights it, a third cuts it, a fourth points it, a fifth grinds it at the top for receiving the head; to make the head requires two or three distinct operations; to put it on, is a peculiar business, to whiten the pins is another; it is even a trade by itself to put them into the paper, and the important business of making a pin, is in this manner, divided up into about eighteen distinct operations, which, in some manufactories, are all performed by distinct hands, though in others the same man will perform two or three of them.* ❞ **(A)**

(Adam Smith, *Wealth of Nations*, 1776)

In a factory we break down the job of making goods, like pins, into many bits. Each worker uses tools and machines to do a special task. We call this the 'division of labour'. The division of labour was a key part of the Industrial Revolution - can you think why? The Industrial Revolution in Britain began in about 1780 and within 50 years Britain had **changed** from having mainly cottage industries to having mainly factory industries. What **evidence** of this change can you see today?

Factory!

What is it like to work in a factory? You can find out by making **envelopes** to put pins into. Then you can write a report on how you might set up a firm to make things.

1 Envelope-making team (AT3)

Split into teams of three or four. Use scrap paper to make envelopes, see **B**. Then judge which team made the best ones, using the grid opposite.

Team	1	2	3	4	5	6	7	8	9	10	11
Number of people in team											
Number of envelopes made											
Quality (mark out of 10)											
Total mark (number of envelopes x quality)											
Mark per team member											

2 The report (AT3, AT1)

Discuss these questions and then write them down with your answers:
• What raw materials do you need?
• Where is the best place to make the envelopes?
• What skills do you need?
• What sort of power do you need - electricity, steam power or just hands?
• Were more envelopes made by people working in groups or by people working on their own?
• Were better-quality envelopes made by people working in groups or on their own?

In your report, note how you would set up your firm; what you would make; how the firm would operate; and the good and bad points about factory industry when compared with cottage industry.

B The envelope game

(1) Make a square shape, fold along the diagonal. Cut off end

(2) Fold corners 1 and 2 to reach beyond centre line of the diagonal at a slight angle

(3) Fold corner 3 so that point reaches well *beyond* centre

(4) Fold point of flap 3 round and under points of flaps 1 and 2

(5) Fold final corner 4 so point reaches *beyond* centre to make flap of envelope

ACTIVITY · ACTIVITY ·

Iron

A perspective view of Coalbrookdale by George Perry and T.Vivares

I love picture **A**. I can almost feel the artist putting down his brush as he finished it. It shows Coalbrookdale - the world's largest centre of industry in 1758. Luckily we have a map from that time to help us work out what the picture shows (**B** is a modern redrawing of it). **C** is an account of Coalbrookdale from the 1750s.

In the year 1700 the whole village consisted of only one furnace, five dwelling houses and a forge or two; about forty years ago the present Iron Foundery was established, and since that time trade and buildings are so far increased that it contains at least 450 inhabitants and finds employment for more than 500 people. **(C)**

(George Perry, quoted in B.Trinder, *The Industrial Revolution in Shropshire*)

Twenty years later Arthur Young, see page 10, came to Coalbrookdale, and left behind a stirring account of what he had seen and heard:

*1776. **Coalbrookdale.** Coalbrookdale itself is a very romantic spot, it is a winding glen between two immense hills which break into various forms, all thickly covered with wood, forming the most beautiful sheets of hanging wood. Indeed too beautiful to be much in unison with that variety of horrors art has spread at the bottom; the noise of the forges, mills etc with their vast machinery, the flames bursting from the furnaces with the burning of the coal and the smoak of the lime kilns.* **(D)**

A famous Quaker family of copper and iron founders, the Darbys, owned Coalbrookdale. Coalbrookdale was rich in coal and in 1709 Abraham Darby had begun to smelt iron, using coke made from coal instead of charcoal made from wood. This early iron was very poor, and could only be cast into moulds to make things like pots, pans and iron girders.

If you visit the world's first iron bridge at Coalbrookdale today, you can see Darby cast-iron still in use. **Cast-iron** had to be reheated, beaten and hammered in a forge into **wrought** iron before it could be used to make tools. At this time firms of iron masters were constantly trying out new ideas to make better-quality iron - can you think why? Factfile **E** lists the main inventions but there were thousands of others.

FACTFILE

Inventions in the iron industry, 1709-1800

Date	Event
1709	Abraham Darby used coke instead of charcoal to smelt iron.
1740-50	Benjamin Huntsman, of Sheffield, invented crucible steel. Huntsman melted bar iron in small clay crucibles in a coke furnace to such a high temperature that the impurities burned away. The steel was hard yet flexible — good for knife blades and springs.
1742	Steam-engines used to pump water back into the furnace pool for powering the bellows to blow the furnace.
1766	First partially successful attempt to use coal in a 'reverbatory' furnace for turning bar iron into wrought iron.
1775	Wilkinson used a steam-engine successfully to blow furnaces.
1783-84	Henry Cort patented his 'puddling' and 'rolling' processes to make wrought iron. The 'puddling' process melted pig-iron with coke, and used metal rods to stir the molten metal. Most of the impurities were burned away. In 'rolling', the purified metal was put through iron rollers which squeezed out remaining impurities.

B

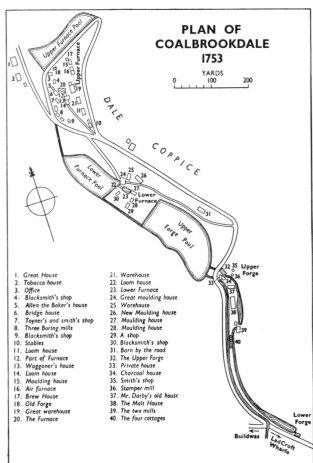

PLAN OF
COALBROOKDALE
1753

YARDS
0   100   200

1. Great House
2. Tobacco house
3. Office
4. Blacksmith's shop
5. Allen the Baker's house
6. Bridge house
7. Toyner's and smith's shop
8. Three Boring mills
9. Blacksmith's shop
10. Stables
11. Loom house
12. Part of Furnace
13. Waggoner's house
14. Loom house
15. Moulding house
16. Air furnace
17. Brew House
18. Old Forge
19. Great warehouse
20. The Furnace
21. Warehouse
22. Loom house
23. Lower Furnace
24. Great moulding house
25. Warehouse
26. New Moulding house
27. Moulding house
28. Moulding house
29. A shop
30. Blacksmith's shop
31. Barn by the road
32. The Upper Forge
33. Private house
34. Charcoal house
35. Smith's shop
36. Stamper mill
37. Mr. Darby's old house
38. The Malt House
39. The two mills
40. The four cottages

History Trail

You have to produce a history trail for visitors to a newly built industrial museum on site **B**. The museum re-creates the history of the early iron industry. Work as a class and on your own, or in pairs or groups.

1 Planning the trail - research (AT3, AT1)
As a class, pool your ideas on the following topics - you can even split them up among you:
• Write down any questions that picture **A** suggests to you, and any facts you can say about it. Say what you might have heard, seen, smelled and felt and what your thoughts might have been on visiting it in 1776. From **B**, work out what the buildings around the upper furnace pool were used for.
• Use **C** and **D** to say what the industrial site might have looked like in 1776, and how it would have grown over the previous 50 years.
• Say how iron making changed between 1700 and 1783 - see **E**.

• Find out where the workers, managers and owners might have lived.
• Carry out an interview with **one** of the figures in **A** about what the area is like and how it might have changed.
• How much trust can you place in sources **A-E**? How would you check what they tell you?

2 Sorting out your ideas (AT1)
Work by yourself or in pairs or threes to plan the things you would include in your trail.

3 Presenting your trail (AT2, AT1)
On a sheet of paper, present your trail in the way you think best. You could do it as a straight piece of factual history, or you could look at it from the point of view of a member of today's Green Party. Make sure that your trail has a heading, and that each part is labelled. The class can choose which one it likes best.

ACTIVITY · ACTIVITY

Iron and Steel

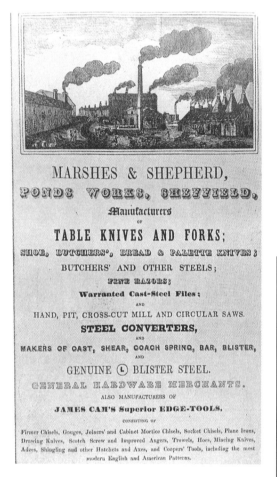

The front page of Marshes and Shepherd's price list for 1838

Your teacher gives you a folder on the history of a Sheffield iron and steel firm, Marshes and Shepherd, containing sources **A-D**. In the mid-nineteenth century the spread of railways and the use of steel to make all machines and tools meant a huge increase in steel output. Marshes and Shepherd was like many other steel firms that grew very quickly and made huge amounts of money from making steel.

What clues does **A** give you about the growth of the iron and steel industry from 1800 to 1900?

Steel Firm!

You have to produce **either** a script **or** a one-side hand-out for a radio programme on the steel industry in the nineteenth century, which re-creates a visit to Marshes and Shepherd in 1858.

1 Finding out (AT3)
• Use **B** and **C** to make a chart of the steel goods that Marshes and Shepherd made. Under each of the following customer headings put the **goods** and **what they were used for.**
Customers: Homes; Other Industries; Shops; Farming; Railways; Armaments.
• In **B** and **C**, what evidence is there of changes in the use of steel?
• Find out about: the inventions of Neilson, Bessemer, Siemens and Gilchrist-Thomas; the Great Exhibition; working in a steel works.

• Work out where Marshes and Shepherd's steel might have been used in your local area in the nineteenth century.

2 The script or hand-out (AT1, AT2)
Base the script on interviews with the owner of Marshes and Shepherd and the workers. Mention: the growth of the firm; changes in making steel; the reasons for the firm's expansion; what the firm made and what these things were used for; what it was like working in the industry.

Pig-iron output 1800-1900	(000 tons)
1800	250
1810	300
1820	450
1830	700
1840	1,300
1850	2,800
1860	4,200
1870	6,400
1880	8,400
1890	7,300 **A**

(Source: P.Deane and W.A.Cole, *British Economic Growth, 1688-1959*, 1969)

The front page of Marshes and Shepherd's price list for 1846

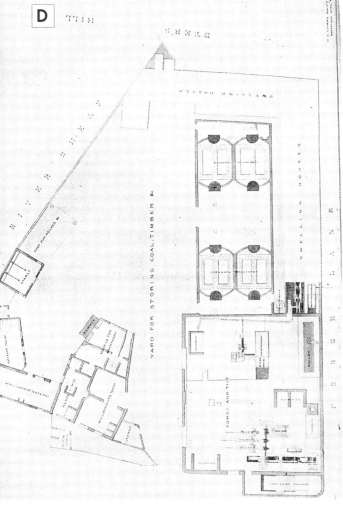

Plan of the firm's steel works

Date	Event
c.1780-1828	Marshes and Shepherd expanded as a firm, making knives, cutlery and other high-grade steel goods in Sheffield. Exported goods mainly to America.
1828	Breakthrough in iron making: **Neilsen's hot blast process** blows hot air through the furnace. Raw coal is used to heat the air, which a steam engine pumps into the furnace. Cuts the amount of fuel used in making iron by half.
1828	Marshes and Shepherd move to new Ponds Works, **D**, where they have a steam-engine, rolling mill, forges and furnaces. Huge growth in company during next 30 years.
1851	At the Great Exhibition of Britain's industrial wealth in 1851, Marshes and Shepherd had on show: 'Specimens of steel used for tools, cutlery, table and small cutlery, butchers' knives, razors' edge tools, files, scythes, hay knife, straw knife, springs for railway trucks, wagons etc.'
1852-53	Firm increases output on new site, and in the **1850s** and **1860s** makes high-quality goods both for armaments and for civilian use. Main export business to North America.
1856	**Bessemer Converter**: new process invented for turning pig-iron into large amounts of steel. Means huge increase in output of steel after 1861, when process spread to all steel works.
1866	A second major advance in steel making: **Siemens's open hearth process.** This was a much cheaper way of making steel than the Bessemer process.
1868	Ponds Works sold to the Midland railway, firm shrinks and concentrates on high-quality steel goods.
1879	Final big advance in iron making: **Gilchrist-Thomas** solves the problem of making good-quality iron from low-grade ore with phosphorus in it.

Steam Power

How often do you see adverts for gas, electricity or petrol? About 150 to 200 years ago the adverts would have been for steam and water power. Just as computers are all the rage today, in 1780 steam-engines were the latest thing. Within 50 years they were to power most of British industry.

Steam-engines were slow to develop. In the early 1700s they had been used to pump mines dry in Cornwall, but these **Newcomen** engines cost a lot to run and were too jerky to use with machines like those used to grind corn and turn lathes. The inventor of the modern steam-engine was **James Watt**. Watt spent all his time trying to make his steam-engines better and better, **A**. James Watt worked with a businessman, Mathew Boulton, who ran the business very well and made sure that Watt's engines were sold all over the world.

In **1769** Watt invented the condenser, which meant that his steam-engine used three times less coal. In **1781** he invented the **rotary** engine. This engine could be linked directly to factory machinery, such as the cotton-spinning 'mule', forge hammers and bellows. From 1781 steam power could now be used to **power all the machines** in a factory, a coal mine or an iron works. Factories could run all year and could be situated near to their source of power (coal) or in places where coal could be sent with ease.

B	Steam power in 1800
Industry	No. using steam power
Wool mills	9
Breweries	12
Canals	18
Copper mines	22
Iron works	28
Coal mines	30
Cotton mills	84

Steam spread to all industries, **B**. In Shropshire, the heart of the Industrial Revolution, about 20 engines were at work in 1781. Their main uses were pumping water from mines and pumping water back into furnace pools. By 1800, with the engines now linked to the machines, the number of steam-engines in Shropshire soared to 200. I picked out clues from an engineer's letters about how steam-engines were used in the Coalbrookdale area:

I examined [looked at] a Steam Engine & the means by which its power was transmitted [sent] to work a pump situated [placed] about 200 yards from it... I applied to young Mr Onions who was at the works, for leave to walk about them... I here examined 4 Steam Engines, one a single Engine ...which works a double blowing cylinder... The other 2 Steam Engines worked the forge hammers by means of cranks and Flywheels... [He goes for a walk] In the way saw two Field Engines such as are now generally used for drawing the coals up from the Pits... [He visits the] Inclined Plane at Coalport by which the boats are taken up from, or let down into a canal close by the side of the river Severn. The length of this Incline was 230 yards & it rose 9 inches in the yard...Steam Engine...is used to work the machinery. (C)

(Letters of Simon Goodrich, December 1799)

The use of steam to power weaving machines meant that by the 1830s the old handloom weavers were no longer able to make a living from weaving cloth. Factories were now widespread and smoke belched from the chimneys that the steam-engines used, **D**. Small, high-pressure steam-engines could be used to power boats and trains. After 1830 this gave the Industrial Revolution a new boost, see pages 26-27.

Steam Engine

You have to prepare a sales poster for our industrial museum, see page 33, to help sell steam-engines in 1830. You can do the work on your own or split up the tasks among your group.

1 Research (AT3, AT1)
The poster should contain facts on the points made in sources **A-C**. Pick out at least one thing from each source that you would like to include in your poster.

2 Design (AT2, AT1)
Design your poster. Think of a heading and a slogan, and the pictures, graphs and maps you want to include. Work out the best ways to get your ideas across and make sure that the layout of the poster has lots of impact.

ACTIVITY · ACTIVITY ·

D

Coal

'I hate museums!' moaned Eleanor as we passed the case packed with a plan of coal mines, **A**; a Davy lamp, **B**; a miner's helmet; a picture of a mine in 1800, **C**; and a factfile on mining, **D**.

Without coal there would have been no Industrial Revolution. Coal was used in many industries, such as brewing, brick making and soap making. When turned into **coke**, coal was a key raw material in making iron and steel, see pages 32-33. Coal heated the water to produce the steam for the steam-engines, which played a huge role in the spread of factories. So we can see that coal was a vital **agent for change**.

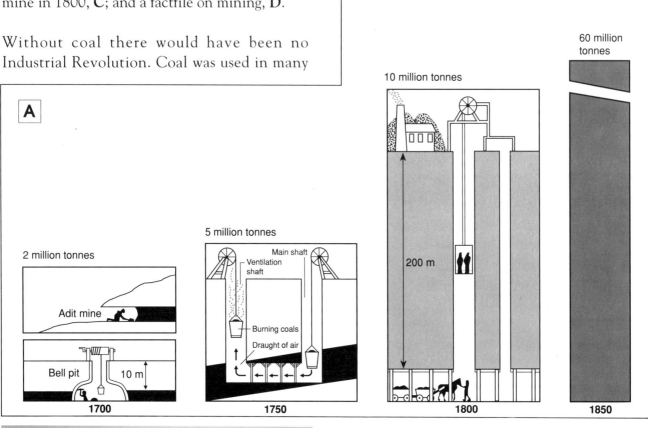

A

2 million tonnes

Adit mine

Bell pit | 10 m

1700

5 million tonnes

Main shaft
Ventilation shaft

Burning coals

Draught of air

1750

10 million tonnes

200 m

1800

60 million tonnes

1850

B

C

a

b

c

d

e

FACTFILE

D

Date	Event
1750+	Big increase in demand for coal because of industry and the use of steam-engines; cutting down of woodland and growth of towns. Coal is a cheap fuel. Horse 'gins' mainly used to wind coal up mine shafts.
1750-1800	New, deep pits increase danger from flooding and 'fire-damp', which caused explosions. Steam-engines used to pump pits dry and raise coal.
1800+	John Buddle's fans for ventilating mines become more commonly used. New, large mines have wagon-ways that use pit ponies.
1815	Humphry Davy invents his safety lamp.
1830s	Use of steel cages to raise coal to surface means a huge increase in output, **A**.

Where coal was mined the landscape changed from green fields to an ugly scene of mine buildings, railroads, steam-engines, spoil heaps and mining cottages. In towns foul coal smoke poured from the chimneys of houses and factories and every building wore a coat of grime. Mining was an awful job - think of working in a dark, cramped, wet space, two or three feet high, either very hot or very cold, and breathing in lungfuls of coal-dust. I found **E** in a government report to give you an idea of what mining meant. If you lived to be 30 years old, you were lucky. And then there were the dreadful accidents - one fire or explosion could mean that a mining town would be full of widows.

E

Mining Museum

You can plan a mining museum using the sources on this page, what you can find in this and other books, and your own ideas. To plan your museum, choose **one** of the tasks below or make up your own, or as a team or class split up the tasks among you. You or your team can compete for the best exhibit or the best plan for the museum - the winners are the ones who get the most class votes. Here are some ideas:

1 Then and now (AT1, AT3)
In three columns put down the main fuel or source of power in 1750, 1900 and today, for the things listed:

	1750	1900	Today
Homes			
Factories			
Road travel			
Boats			
Lighting			
Farm work			

2 Designing an improved safety lamp (AT3, AT1)
The Davy Lamp, **B**, had a metal gauze filter in front of the lamp's flame, which cooled the flame and stopped it from lighting the gas coming from the coal-face. Draw a plan for a better lamp using modern materials.

3 Title/caption (AT3)
Produce a title, a caption and labels for picture **E** to explain what it shows.

4 Environment (AT2)
You are a member of today's Green Party. Produce a title, a caption and labels for **C** to explain what the picture shows at **a-e** and list what steps you would take to protect the environment.

5 Interview (AT1)
Write an interview between the woman in **E** and a mines inspector looking into working conditions.

6 Fact lines (AT1)
Produce a headline of 10 words or fewer for each of the main points in factfile **D**, and a headline for a mining disaster in mine **C** in 1800.

ACTIVITY · ACTIVITY

Cotton

1812. Ruin stared John Heathcoat in the face - the rioters had wrecked his cotton factory. He couldn't go on, he would have to leave and make a new start. So he trekked from the Midlands to Devon and set up a new cotton-spinning firm, Heathcoats. Today it is still the main source of work in Tiverton, Devon.

By 1812 Britain had seen 30 years of rapid growth in the cotton industry. What were the reasons or **causes** of this **change**? **A** is my list of background factors, while factfile **C** shows the main inventions that changed cotton from a **cottage** industry to a **factory** industry.

A key to the growth of cotton was the **role of entrepreneurs** - the men who ran the cotton firms. Without them there would have been no Industrial Revolution. The most famous entrepreneur was Sir Richard Arkwright.

I made up the game 'King Cotton' to show why cotton firms like John Heathcoat's and Richard Arkwright's might make money and grow or go bust. Play the game to learn about these causes. The game is based on facts I found in history books. As a class, you can be up to 40 cotton firms competing against each other.

A **Why the cotton industry grew in the north of England**

• The proximity [closeness] of the Pennines meant that there was **plenty of water power** for cotton-spinning factories. Later, local coalfields meant that there was fuel for steam-engines.

• There were a large number of **skilled spinners and weavers** from the old wool cottage industry who could now switch to factory work.

• The **lime-free water** and **damp climate** were good for stretching and spinning cotton thread.

• The **port of Liverpool** was perfect for sending cotton goods abroad, and for importing raw cotton. Turnpike roads, canals and then railways made it easy to take the cotton thread and cloth to market and bring raw materials to the factory.

• There was a **good supply of raw cotton** from India, and later America, to meet the huge demand for cotton goods.

• There were **plenty of businessmen** with the skill, knowledge and drive to set up cotton firms.

• There was **enough money** in local banks and in private hands to invest in setting up cotton firms.

• In **1774** there was the **repeal of a heavy tax** charged on cotton thread and cloth made in Britain.

• **Britain was the first country** to spin cotton in a factory.

• There was a **huge increase in demand** for cotton goods:

a. because of the great rise in the number of people living in Britain

b. because the price of cotton cloth dropped sharply (a huge amount of cloth was made, the price of raw cotton fell and transport costs fell)

c. cotton clothes became fashionable.

FACTFILE

C	
Main inventions in the spinning industry	

Date	Event
1733	John Kay invented the **Flying Shuttle**. Hammers were fixed to the weaving loom to knock the shuttle from side to side.
1765	James Hargreaves invented the **Spinning Jenny, B**. Try and work out how the Jenny worked! The number of threads it could spin rose quickly from 6 to 80 by the mid-1780s.
1769	Richard Arkwright patented the **Water Frame**. Water power was used to spin a thread strong enough for both the warp (down thread) and the weft (cross thread). Water Frames were perfect for factories.
1779	**Crompton's Mule, D**. This was a machine that took the best ideas from the Jenny and the Water Frame and used them to spin a cotton thread better than anything else available at that time. What does **D** suggest about how cotton-spinning has changed from **B**? Why did the Mule help the cotton boom?
1780s	Thomas Bell invented a machine for printing cotton cloth. What things could now be made out of cotton?
1790s	Spread of steam-engines to cotton factories. Cotton making could now happen near coalfields as well as near rivers. What might this mean for the growth of the cotton industry?
1800s	The spread of chemical bleaches and dyes meant bleaching, dyeing and printing could happen in one place. Where?
1812	Invention of the first good weaving machine for use in factories - **Roberts's Power Loom**. All stages in the making of cotton cloth could now take place in a single factory.

King Cotton

1 Playing the game (AT1)
The game is on page 42. The year is 1780.
a Place a counter in the 'start square'. Each square tells you the challenge facing your firm. Before you decide what to do in each square, cover up the 'heads' and 'tails' columns, which give an idea of the consequences of your decisions. Each round represents five years.
b Then toss a coin to see how you have done, ie. heads or tails. You can only leave the start square when you have raised the money needed to start your firm.
c Make an entry in your firm's diary for each round.
d In a 'credit/debit' column enter the amount of money you make, lose or owe in each round. When your debit is bigger than your credit you have gone bust - start again.
e For the next round, move from the square you are in to the next numbered square - 1 to 2, 2 to 3, and so on.
f The winner is the firm that makes the most money!

2 Expanding the game (AT1, AT2)
At the end of the game make up **two** more squares, based on the facts in **C** about changes in weaving cotton thread into cloth.

3 Report (AT1)
Write a letter to the people who lent you money to build the factory, saying how well your firm did, and give the reasons why.

41

SQUARE 1

You are going to set up a cotton-spinning mill in 1780. You need £300. How will you raise the money? Will you: a. try and raise money from 20 local farmers, landowners, estate agents and wool merchants OR b. approach a bank in London?

Use a coin - H = Heads, T = Tails **OR**
Use a dice - H = 1-3 on a dice, T = 4-6

1a **H** You manage to raise the money. Put £300 in the 'credit' column of your accounts.

T There is a run on the county bank. You cannot raise the money.

1b **H** The bank puts up the money.

T The bank refuses as it thinks your business is a bad risk.

SQUARE 2

*What **spinning machines** will you buy? You will need 10: a. Water Frames OR b. Mules.*

2a **H** You buy the Water Frames, and they run well. The firm makes £200 profit.

T There is a glut of cotton being spun, Water Frames make a low-quality thread, you lose £100.

2b **H** The Mules are a great success, and you are £300 in pocket.

T Crompton sues you, claiming your machines are copies of his. The case costs you £300.

SQUARE 3

*A **sales plan** is vital - you must get your goods to market quickly and at a low cost. Will you choose: a. Europe OR b. America, as your main market?*

3a **H** Your American agents report huge orders, the factory is working flat out. You make £300.

T War has broken out with America. Losses mount - £350 in all.

3b **H** The European market is booming, the factory is working day and night - £300 profit.

T War with France, the French seize a ship with all your output in it. You lose £350.

SQUARE 4

*What will you do with your profits? Will you: a. **invest** them **all** in new methods OR b. put the money in the bank?*

4a **H** You make a breakthrough in spinning, and your new thread earns you £400.

T There is nothing to show for the money spent, you lose it all and owe £100.

4b **H** The money is safe in the bank and earns £100 in interest.

T There is a run on the bank, you lose ALL your money.

SQUARE 5

*You have raised £500 to invest. Do you: a. spend it on hiring the **best factory manager** and **accountant** you can find OR b. spend it on **reorganising the factory's machinery** and buying new, better Mules to increase output?*

5a **H** Your new manager and accountant give the factory a new lease of life - profits soar, and you make £400.

T The manager's new ideas do not go down well with your workers, output falls and you lose your main contracts. Lose up to £500, ie. the money you have up to that amount.

5b **H** The factory runs much more efficiently with the new layout of machines and new, improved Mules. You have 12 spinning machines where there were 10 before and you employ fewer workers. Profits rise to £700.

T While the machines are being put in, a fire breaks out and you lose ALL your money.

SQUARE 6

The factory needs to recruit 100 new workers. Do you: a. give them a thorough training OR b. give them the bare amount you think they will need to work the machines?

6a **H** The factory runs very well and your output increases - £300 profit.

T The workers go on strike and demand higher wages, you lose £400.

6b **H** The factory continues to make money although output is not high - £100 profit.

T The Luddites, see page 48, attack your factory and, with the help of your workers, burn it down - £500 loss.

Cotton Town

By 1830 cotton firms spun and wove cotton in steam-powered factories. Cotton towns and cities mushroomed, creating a new landscape of terraced houses and hundreds of smoke-belching factory chimneys.

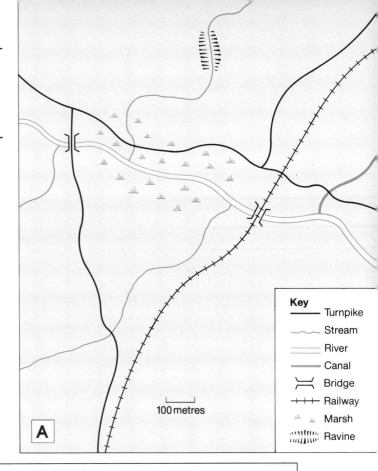

Model Maker

You get a job working for a model-making firm that has decided to compete for the job of making a model of a nineteenth-century cotton town for an industrial museum. Your firm will have to give a plan of its model to the museum. The plans will be put on public display and judged. Work on your own, in pairs or small groups.

1 Research (AT3, AT1)
The model has to stick to the rules that the mill owner would have used to build a real town. Find out what you can about nineteenth-century towns and cotton mills.

2 Planning the town and factory (AT1, AT2)
The model will be built on site **A.** Work out where you will put the features in **the order shown** in the key below. You can photocopy them, cut them out and move them around **A**. You can add other features you find out about in your research - but make sure they are to the right scale.

3 Factory rules (AT2)
Factory workers had to obey strict rules because working in a factory was very different from working on the land or in cottage industry or as a servant. Can you think why? Draw up a set of factory rules to go with the model.

4 Labelling the model (AT1)
For each part of the model, write out a label which explains why it has been placed on that part of the site, and what its role is. Prepare a talk to explain the thinking behind your design.

KEY		
Weir		- on the river, near flat land for mills and close to where railway crosses the river and the canal joins it
Spinning and Weaving Mill		- next to the river on area of flat land, downstream from the weir
Bleaching Mill		- on a mill race below the weir
Dye House	factory	- next to Spinning and Weaving Mill, on the mill race
Warehouse		- between Spinning and Weaving Mill and the Dye House
School		- near the factory
Apprentices' House (girls and boys)		- near the factory
Factory Owner's Great House		- overlooking the mills, on high land
Cottages for 100 families		- close to the factory
Gasometer		- on the railway line
Railway sidings		- from the railway line to the factory

ACTIVITY · ACTIVITY ·

43

Wedgwood

The Government is very keen on teaching young people how to make money from buying, making and selling things, both **goods** and **services**. If you want to start your own firm you can learn from great figures of the past, such as Arkwright, the cotton king; Watt, the steam-engine maker; and Wedgwood, the potter. What were the reasons or **causes** of their success? What changes did they bring about? How did their work as industrialists tie in with background factors, such as the development of new kinds of roads [turnpikes] and canals, discoveries in science, the opening up of new markets for their goods and having savings to invest in their firms? Could you do as well as they did?

To me Wedgwood has always been the great success story of the Industrial Revolution - a first-class businessman or **entrepreneur**. Below are some reasons for his success - how many of these points can you spot in factfile **A**? I found sources **C-F** in books on Wedgwood.

A FACTFILE

Date	Event
1730	Born at Burslem, Staffordshire. His father was a potter. As a boy, he trained as a potter.
1759	Had saved enough money to set up his own pottery.
1760s	Carried out lots of experiments into making better pots. His 'Queen's ware' was a great success.
1760s	Backed turnpike and canal building plans, **B**. (It cost 5p a mile to send a load of pots to market.)
1768	Teamed up with Bentley, a merchant, who was able to tell him how to sell his pots.
1769	Opened Europe's biggest pottery factory at Etruria.
1777	Trent-Mersey canal opened. Perfect for carrying his pots to market and bringing clay to his factory. Cost of sending pots to market dropped from 5p to 1p a mile.
1780s	Sold famous dinner service to the Empress of Russia. Boulton and Watt steam-engines in use at Etruria.

Reasons for Wedgwood's success

- **High standards** He had close control over the making of his pots. He made sure that each piece was perfect.
- **Factory system** He broke down the making of pots into parts, and made sure that his workers were trained to carry out these tasks.
- **Craftsmen** He used first-class craftsmen to paint and glaze his pots.
- **Research** He spent a lot of time and money working on new kinds of pots, glazes and patterns.
- **Management** He ran his factory well and made sure that it was planned along the best lines.
- **Sales** Selling his pots was a key part of his firm's growth. He pushed both home sales and exports. He set up London, Bath and Dublin showrooms, only open to the upper class. He **advertised** widely - people bought his pots because of their 'snob appeal'. He kept a tight grip on his sales force.
- **Transport** Turnpikes and canals meant that he could get his pots to market on time with fewer breakages, and get raw materials to his factory easily.
- **Partners** Wedgwood had a partner, Thomas Bentley, who played a key role in his business. He looked after the selling of Wedgwood's pots.

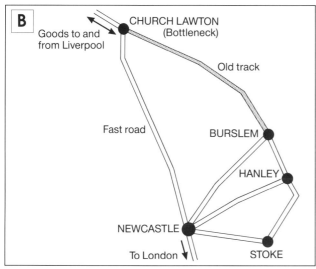

Between Burslem and Church Lawton was a rutted, muddy track so pots going to Liverpool had to go through Newcastle. What do you think Wedgwood did to get his goods quickly and safely to Liverpool?

What does this source suggest about how Wedgwood kept control over the making of his pots? Invent a speech bubble dialogue between Wedgwood and the worker in this picture.

66 *You will see the vast importance in most manufactures [making things] of making the greatest quantity possible in a given time. Rent goes on whether we make much or little. Wages to the Boys and Odd [job] Men, Warehouse Men and bookkeepers, who are a kind of satellite to the [pot] makers are nearly the same whether we make twenty dozen of vases or ten dozen per week. The cost of modelling and moulds, and the expense of sale, would not be much increased if we could sell double the quantity at our rooms in Town [London], which lowering some of the markets may enable us to do.* 99 **(D)**

66 *Be so good as to let me know what is going on in the great world. How many lords and dukes visit your [show] rooms, praise your beauties, thin your shelves and fill your purses.* 99 **(E)**

(**D** and **E** are from a letter to Thomas Bentley from Josiah Wedgwood, 1771)

66 *1771. Mr Wedgwood engages [agrees] that every piece shall be delivered whole at their houses in any part of England, or if any of the goods are broke, the deficiency [breakage] shall be made up either in goods or by deducting [taking away] so much from the bill, at the option [wish] of the purchaser [buyer], who shall likewise be at liberty [free] to return the whole, or any part of the goods they ordered [Wedgwood will pay the cost of return] if they do not find them agreeable to their wishes [like them].* 99 **(F)**

(A newspaper advert)

Entrepreneur - Young Enterprise Scheme

You have to work out a business plan to set up a firm which will design, make and sell a clay object of your choice. You can work on your own or with partners. Your plan will be based on the reasons why Wedgwood succeeded.

1 Research (AT3, AT1)
Make out a table with three columns:
Cause   Source   Comment

Look at each cause in the table on Wedgwood's success, write it down in the first column and then find which source or sources link to it. In the comment column put down what the source tells you about the cause.

2 Design
Design your clay object, and then plan how you will make it.

3 The business plan
Make out a business plan for setting up your firm in fewer than 500 words, as a bid for money to start it. Present your ideas to your class as if they were the manager of the local bank. Then they decide whether they would advance you the money to start your business.

· ACTIVITY · ACTIVITY ·

Speenhamland

D

Each week seems to bring a bright new idea about what to do with those who have lost their jobs - the unemployed. Unemployment is not a new problem. Let's go back 200 years to see how they coped then. Each of England's 11,000 parishes had to look after its own poor. In 1795 local magistrates or JPs, often rich farmers like William Hurrell (see pages 10-11), were at their wits' end to try and stop the poor from starving to death. The harvest was very bad. There was not enough food to eat and the starving were rioting across England. I chose this stark report on a Devon parish to show the problem:

66 *No labourer can at present maintain himself, wife and children on his earnings. All have relief from the parish in money, or corn at a reduced price. Before the war wheaten bread and cheese, and about twice a week meat, were their usual food; now barley bread and no meat. They have of late made great use of potatoes. An industrious healthy man can earn 8s a week by piece work [weaving cloth] on average throughout the year. Labourer's children are often bound out as apprentices [unpaid workers] at 8 years of age to the farmers. Prior to the present scarcity a labourer, if his wife was healthy, could maintain two young children on his 6s a week and liquor without any parochial [parish] relief.* 99 **(A)**

(Sir Frederick Eden, *The State of the Poor*, 1797)

If a person was too old or sick to look after him or herself, that person would have to go and live in the local workhouse. The JPs had the local **poor rate** to spend on the poor, but they wanted to keep it as low as possible. People hated paying taxes then as much as we do now! At Speenhamland in Berkshire, the county's JPs met at the Pelican Inn. They had a brain wave, and for their parishes they decided:

66 *That the present state of the Poor does require further assistance than has been generally given them. [They agreed that]*

When the Gallon Loaf of Second Flour weighing 8lb 11oz [4 kilograms] shall cost 1s:

Then every poor and industrious man shall have for his own support 3s weekly, either produced by his own or his family's labour, or an allowance from the poor rates, and for the support of his wife and every other of his family, 1s 6d.

When the Gallon Loaf shall cost 1s 4d:

Then every poor and industrious man shall have 4s weekly for his own and 1s 10d for the support of every other of his family.

And so in proportion, as the price of bread rise or falls (that is to say) 3d to the man, and a 1d to every other of the family, on every 1d which the loaf rises above 1s. 99 **(B)**

(English Historical Documents)

Their plan for keeping the poor alive became known as the **Speenhamland System**. It spread like wildfire - can you think why? For the rest of the Napoleonic Wars (1793-1815) grain prices were high. Farmers were well off and farm workers just had enough to live on, but in years of bad weather, such as 1810-11, they could starve.

After 1815 farm wages stayed low in the south of England, but the new factory towns in the north of England kept northern farm workers' pay up because factories were always looking for workers and paid well. Again there were bad farming years, such as 1823, when foul weather meant little or no work for farm workers and poor crops. I read through William Cobbett's *Rural Rides* to find an account of how awful things were:

66 *A man had a sledge-hammer, and was cracking the heads of the big stones that had been laid on the road a good while ago. This is a very good way, but this man told me, that he was set at this, because the farmers had no employment for many of the men. "Well," said I, "but they pay you to do this!" "Yes," he said. "Well, then," said I, "is it not better for them to pay you for working on their land?" Yet, at a season like this, the farmers are so poor as to be unable to pay the labourers to work on the land!* 99 **(C)**

(William Cobbett, Rural Rides, 1830)

By 1830 most counties in England had brought in the Speenhamland System to keep workers alive when bread prices rose sharply. Historians argue about whether the Agricultural Revolution meant an increase in the number of poor, or whether, in fact, it made lots of new jobs for farm workers. But all agree that in a bad farming year the life of the farm labourer and his family, **D**, could become one of hunger, despair and death.

Speenhamland!

As an investigative reporter, write a story **either** for *The Times* in 1830 as a fan of the Speenhamland System, seeing it as the only way of stopping the poor from starving **or** for a radical newspaper like *The Red Dwarf* (see page 51) as Speenhamland's bitter enemy, arguing that it keeps the poor's wages at starvation level.

1 Research - coping with the poor (AT3)
• Use source **A** to work out a day's menu for a labourer's family before the Napoleonic Wars and in **1795**.
• Find out from **A-C** how JPs might have treated an unemployed farm worker's family like the one in **D** - John Scott and his wife, Mary, and their three children, James, aged 12, Elizabeth, aged 8, Fred, aged 4, and their grand-mother - in 1830.

2 The form (AT1)
• Using the headings below, make out a form for your newspaper showing what can be done with the parish poor.
Headings: the name of your parish; the date; all the members of your family - father, mother, children, dependants, ie. grandparent; decisions about what to do with them.
• Then fill in the form for your own family as if you were: **a)** earning 9s (45p) a week and the price of flour is 1s 6d (7.5p) or **b)** your family is out of work.

3 The parish meeting (AT1, AT3)
As a class, you can hold an 1830 meeting of the local parish council to decide how you are going to deal with the poor of the parish using the Speenhamland System.

4 Two views of Speenhamland - reporting the meeting (AT2)
Produce your report arguing **either** for **or** against the Speenhamland System.

Ned Lud

A

How old are you? Abraham Charlson was 12 years old in May 1812. The tears streamed down his face as he cried out for his mother, and then he was hanged, **A**. Why? **B-D** are brief extracts from the time which throw light on Abraham's fate and **E** is a factfile on Luddism. Abraham was a Luddite. The term 'Luddism' came from 'Ned Lud' - the signature that appeared on public letters complaining about the spread of new machines.

> *[On the 29 April 1812, fourteen men and boys were tried for] having wilfully and maliciously set on fire and burnt a weaving mill, warehouse and loomshop in possession of Thomas Rowe and Thomas Duncough, at Westhoughton.* **(B)**

(Trial record, Lancaster, May 1812)

> *He [Abraham Charlson] had a scythe on a pole, getting straw from a barn and taking it inside the mill.* **(C)**

(Evidence given at his trial at Lancaster, May 1812)

> *Your factory and all that it Contains Will and Shall Surely Be Set on fire it is Not our Desire to Do you the Least Injury But We are fully Determin'd to Destroy Both Dressing Machines and Steam Looms Let Who Will be the Owners.* **(D)**

(Letter, 19 April 1812)

FACTFILE

E

Date	Event
1811	Trade crisis because of the war with Napoleon. Many factories shut down. Workers were also afraid that new machines for making cloth would mean lost jobs.
1812	**March-April** High bread prices and the threat of losing jobs from new machines led Yorkshire Luddites to attack factories. Lancashire Luddites rioted in towns such as Manchester, Oldham and Rochdale. 12,000 troops could not stop them. **24 April** Luddites burnt down Westhoughton mill. **May** Trial of Luddites in Lancaster. Unrest spread across England. Reports of Luddite plans to rise against the Government. Things stayed tense throughout summer. Abraham Charlson was hanged.
1813	Luddism died down.

A Luddite History Trial

You can stage your own Luddite trial **or** prepare a poster for **either** the defence **or** prosecution of Abraham Charlson. The class can be the jury in the trial **or** they can judge which poster is the best. Take turns to put your case.

1 Sorting out the facts (AT3)
- What crime did Abraham commit?
- What evidence is there that he burned down the mill?
- What does source **D** prove?

2 Defence or prosecution (AT1, AT2)
- **Either** as a prosecutor **or** as a defender of Abraham, jot down any ideas that **B-D** give you about what Abraham might have been doing when the mill burned down.
- In turn, interview witnesses for either the prosecution or the defence.
- Then vote on whether he was guilty or not.

3 The poster (AT2)
Produce your own poster on Luddism and Abraham's fate.

ACTIVITY · ACTIVITY

Peterloo

Amritsar, Bloody Sunday, Peterloo, Sharpeville, Tiananmen Square - these names live on in our minds because many think they were massacres of innocent people. One of these, Peterloo, took place in Manchester, England, in August 1819.

After the Napoleonic Wars there was a slump in industry. Thousands were out of work and living on poor relief, see pages 46-47, or had taken a cut in wages. In 1817-18 many workmen in the north of England pushed for the reform of Parliament through their Political Unions. They backed parliamentary reform as a way of ending the misery. The Political Unions organised over 2,000 reform petitions to Parliament.

Eric Evans, a famous history professor, tells us about Peterloo:

What turned out to be the symbolic climax [high point] of the peaceful assembly [meetings] method of protest occurred in Manchester in August 1819. The mass meeting at St Peter's fields was the fourth organised in large cities that summer, coming after expressions [shows] of popular feeling [support] for parliamentary reform in Birmingham, Leeds and London. About 60,000 people, including many women and children, attended the Manchester meeting. The arrest of the main speaker, Orator Hunt, and the forcible dispersal [break up] of the assembly by the sabres of the local yeomanry [cavalry] at the instigation [request] of the local magistracy [JPs] was a panic reaction [response]. **(A)**

(Eric Evans, *The Forging of the Modern State*, 1983)

About 11 people died in the cavalry charge. Source **B** is part of a cartoon from the time.

B

Peterloo

You can turn **B** into a postcard showing the viewpoint of **either** a radical reformer **or** a government supporter, **or** write a folk-song about the massacre.

1 Sorting out your ideas (AT3, AT1)
Think about these questions:
* Who was Henry Hunt?
* What message is on the banners in **B**?
* Why might workmen back reform in 1817-18?
* What events led up to Peterloo?
* What point is the cartoonist trying to make?

2 The postcard (AT2)
* Fill in speech bubbles from the mouths of the numbered people in the picture as if the postcard was **either** for or against the Government's attack on the crowd.
* Produce a title or caption for the card.
* On the back of the card write a message as if you were talking **either** to woman **1 or** to soldier **2**.
* **Or** write a folk-song about the massacre from **one** of the two viewpoints above. Read or sing your songs to the class.

ACTIVITY · ACTIVITY ·

Captain Swing

66 *About three o'clock in the morning of yesterday week I was awakened by the blowing of a horn... Myself and my brother got out of bed. I looked through the window: we have no upstairs. A great many persons came before the house and holloed to us to unlock the door or they would beat it open. I opened the door. Three or four came in. They said if we did not go with them they would draw us out. My brother and I went out with them into the street... All the houses were visited and the men in them pressed.* 99 **(A)**

(Evidence of a swing rioter, 23 November 1830)

66 *Remember in Kent they have set 'with fire' all that would not submit and you will serve the same for we are determined to make you support the Poor better than they have been soppored yet for they are all starving at present so pull down your Thrashing Mashine or els Bread or Fire without delay. For we are 5 thousand men and will not be stopt.* 99 **(B)**

(Swing letter to a farmer, 17 November 1830)

66 *His [the farmer's] premises were attacked first yesterday morning Sunday about 2 o'clock by about 30 men who said they had been sent to his house to destroy his threshing machine. [The mob leaves, but comes back at 11.] A large mob of upwards of 200 persons returned to the premises, broke open the barn and entirely destroyed the machine.* 99 **(C)**

(The farmer's evidence, 21 November 1830)

66 *Da-n, let it burn, I wish it was the house; we can warm ourselves now; we only want some potatoes; there is a nice fire to cook them by.* 99 **(D)**

(Report of a rioter's comment in *The Times*, September 1830)

A-G are some sources I found in a book on the Swing Riots of 1830-32. The rioters smashed threshing machines and burned hayricks and barns full of corn. Factfile **H** helps to make sense of sources **A-G**.

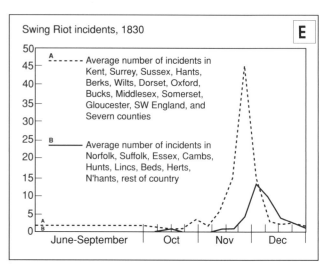

Swing Riot incidents, 1830 — **E**

A - - - - Average number of incidents in Kent, Surrey, Sussex, Hants, Berks, Wilts, Dorset, Oxford, Bucks, Middlesex, Somerset, Gloucester, SW England, and Severn counties

B ——— Average number of incidents in Norfolk, Suffolk, Essex, Cambs, Hunts, Lincs, Beds, Herts, N'hants, rest of country

June-September | Oct | Nov | Dec

(Source: E. Hobsbawm, *Captain Swing*)

PUBLIC NOTICE.

THE *Magistrates* in the Hundreds of *Tunstead* and *Happing*, in the County of Norfolk, having taken into consideration the disturbed state of the said Hundreds and the Country in general, wish to make it publicly known that *it is their opinion* that such disturbances principally arise from the use of Threshing Machines, and to the insufficient Wage of the Labourers. The Magistrates therefore beg to *recommend* to the Owners and Occupiers of Land in these Hundreds, to *discontinue the use of Threshing Machines, and to increase the Wages of Labour to Ten Shillings* a week for able bodied men, and that when task work is preferred, that it should be put out at such a rate as to enable an industrious man to earn Two Shillings per day.

The Magistrates are determined to enforce the Laws against all tumultuous Rioters and Incendiaries, and they look for support to all the respectable and well disposed part of the Community; at the same time they feel a full Conviction, that *no severe measures will be necessary* if the proprietors of Land will give proper employment to the Poor on their own Occupations, and encourage their Tenants to do the same.

SIGNED,

JOHN WODEHOUSE.
W. R. ROUS.
J. PETRE.
GEORGE CUBITT.
WILLIAM GUNN.
W. F. WILKINSON.
BENJAMIN CUBITT.
H. ATKINSON.

North Walsham,
24th November, 1830.

F

J. PLUMBLY, PRINTER, NORTH WALSHAM.

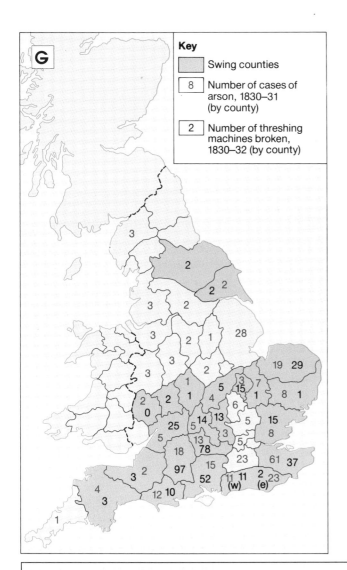

G Key

▨	Swing counties
8	Number of cases of arson, 1830–31 (by county)
2	Number of threshing machines broken, 1830–32 (by county)

Date	Event
1815	The Government put an import tax, the **Corn Laws**, on grain coming in to Britain to keep up the price of bread.
1816-17 & 1822	Years of high bread prices and a rise in labourers out of work. Outbreaks of rick burning, cattle maiming and farm burning.
1829 & 1830	Poor harvests, high price of bread, low wages and a rise in the number of unemployed farm workers.
1830	**June-December:** spread of riots of farm labourers across southern England, **E**. Rioters demanded: higher wages; the destruction of threshing machines which threatened winter work for farm labourers; and provision of work, food and money for the local poor. Rioters visited farms, burning hayricks and barns and wrecking threshing machines. They claimed their leader was 'Captain Swing'.
1831	Riots continued. Over 2,000 rioters arrested, 600 jailed, 500 transported to Australia and 19 hanged.

Wanted - Swing Rioters!

Produce a 'wanted' poster for swing rioters in November 1831. **Or** on your own, in pairs or in groups, prepare a children's history page on the Swing Riots for **one** of two modern newspapers, *The Red Dwarf* or *The Truth*. *The Red Dwarf* is a left-wing, radical newspaper that backs workers' rights, women's rights and the Green Party. *The Truth* is a right-wing paper which supports big business and thinks that strikes should be banned. You have to prepare a front page.

1 Questions (AT1)
As a reporter, what questions will you ask about the Swing Riots?

2 Sorting out the facts (AT3)
Work through the sources and anything else you can find out about the Swing Riots, and note down answers that you find to your questions.

3 The front page (AT2, AT1)
On your front page you could have:

- A **banner headline** - making the point that the newspaper is trying to put across to its readers.
- A **cartoon** that gives your view of the riots, based on facts in **A-F**.
- **Interviews** with farmers, landowners and rioters on what is happening.
- A **map** to show the spread of the riots.
- The paper's **comment column**, putting its views on the Swing Riots.
- A **public statement** on the riots from either swing rioters or landlords.
- A **'wanted' broadsheet** like F, with details of the rioters in C and offering a reward for their arrest.
- A **Swing Riot crossword puzzle.**
- A **Swing Riot factfile.**

4 Presentation (AT2)
You can produce your **history page** on a large sheet of paper, and then put the page on display **or** you can put your poster on display. The class can then judge which are the best pages and posters.

ACTIVITY · ACTIVITY ·

The Poor Law

Do you like school? How about this for your first day at a special kind of boarding school (you arrive with your parents):

None of us wanted to go, but we must go, and so we came to our big home. The very vastness of it chilled us, [B]. Our entry was more chilling still. Everybody we saw and spoke to looked as if made from metal, as if worked from within by a hidden machinery. Their voices were metallic, and sounded harsh and demanding. The younger ones huddled more close to their parents, as if from fear of these stern officials... We at last landed in a cellar, clean and bare, and as grim as I have since seen in prison cells. We were told this was the place where we should have to be washed and put on our workhouse clothes. Nobody asked us if we were tired, or if we had had any breakfast. **(A)**

Now for your school uniform:

We youngsters were roughly undressed, roughly and coldly washed and roughly dressed in rough clothes. Our under clothes were all covered up by a rough linen pinafore. Then we parted amid bitter cries, the young ones were taken one way and the parents (shut up too) were taken as well to different parts of that merciful place. We might have carried out some awful crime or had some dreadful disease. **(C)**

And on to the main school and dining room:

I was taken or shoved into a large room which I found was both dining and schoolroom. I saw hungry looking lads with secret glances. I saw a stern, military, corpse-like man who was said to be

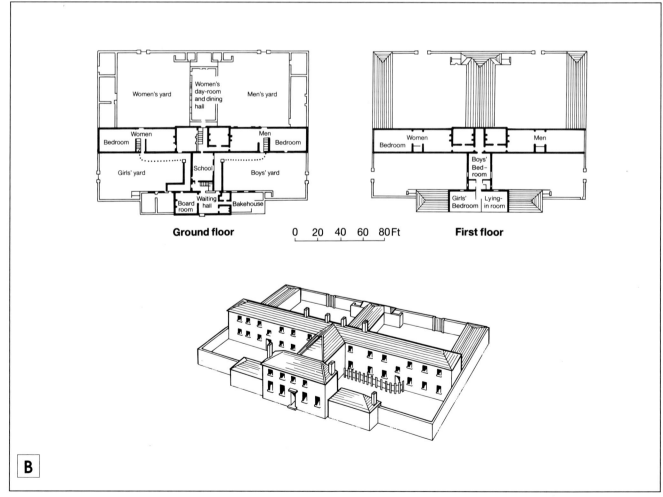

Ground floor   0 20 40 60 80 Ft   **First floor**

B

Plans for a new workhouse

the schoolmaster. I noticed his chilling glances carrying menace in every look. **(D)**

I came across the story of Chell workhouse years ago, and it still fills me with horror. What might your lessons have been like? I was lucky to find this account of a workhouse lesson for infants, taken from Charles Dickens' magazine, *Household Words*, in 1850:

❝ **T** *"What day is this?"* **P** *"Monday."* **T** *"What sort of a day is it?"* **P** *"Very fine."* **T** *"Why is it a fine day?"* **P** *"Because the sun shines, and it does not rain."* **T** *"Is rain a bad thing, then?"* **P** *"No."* **T** *"What is it useful for?"* **P** *"To make the flowers and the fruit grow."* **T** *"Who sends rain and sunshine?"* **P** *"God."* **T** *"What ought we to do in return for his goodness?"* **P** *"Praise him."*

"Let us praise him, then" added the master. And the children, all together, repeated and then sung a part of the 49th Psalm … A lesson on morals succeeded, which seemed to interest the children. It was partly in the form of a tale told by the master. A gentleman who was kind to the poor, went to visit in gaol a boy imprisoned for crime. The restraint of the gaol, and the shame of the boy, were so described, as to impress the children with strong interest. Then the boy's crime was traced to disobedience, and the excellence of obedience to teachers and parents was shown.❞ **(E)**

(Charles Dickens, *Household Words*, 13 July 1850)

As well as learning to read, write, do sums and study the Bible, the older children spent three to four hours a day gardening or learning a craft, such as shoe making or carpentry. The workhouse was where out-of-work men, women, children, the sick and the old who had no-one to look after them were forced to go.

Before 1830 the cost of looking after the poor had soared. This fact and the Swing Riots forced the Government to act. They asked experts to find out what was going on and then tell the Government what to do. The experts said:

• the Government should stop the **outdoor relief** of the Speenhamland System to all those who could work and were under 60 years old

• **all** out-of-work people who were not ill or crippled should live in the workhouse with less to eat than the lowest-paid worker

• new workhouses should be built for groups of parishes

• families in the workhouse should be split up into groups of men, women and children.

The **Poor Law Amendment Act of 1834** carried out these plans. But in factory towns where huge numbers of men and women lost their jobs in slumps, the new Poor Law was a disaster - can you think why? Outdoor relief carried on, but working people hated the new Poor Law. They fought tooth and nail to stay out of the workhouse. In 1902 a House of Commons report said that none of 34 people who had died of hunger had ever asked to go into the workhouse.

The Workhouse Drama

You can use **A-E** to help you work out a drama of life in the workhouse.

1 Researching the scenes (AT3)
Study **A-E** to work out ideas about the following scenes and any others you can think of:
• being out of work, sick or old
• going to the workhouse
• being washed and clothed
• hearing the rules for pauper children in the workhouse
• school lessons - what part did religion play?
• mealtimes; work; going to bed
• rioters attacking the workhouse
• flashback - comparing the workhouse school with a day in your own school.

2 The characters (AT1)
• Work out who will be in your drama.
• Split up the scenes among you. Then take one scene and decide what is happening. Write the outline of your scene and sketch what it might look like.

3 Presentation - the drama (AT2)
Act out, write up or present your ideas for your scene of the play.

Factory Reform

Millions of children like you are almost slaves. You have found out about such slavery from clues **A-E**. Now you have a chance on a local children's TV programme to tell what you know. **A** and **B** are eye-witness accounts of visits to a pin factory and a pipe works. **C** tells you what working in a cotton factory did to Robert Blincoe, a poor orphan with no-one to look after him. For 14 years he was a child slave, an apprentice in a cotton mill. I came across **D** and **E** which show what it was like to work in a brick works and in a 'sweat shop'.

66 *30 November 1840. Visit to Messrs Phipsons' Pin Factory, Birmingham... The children who head the pins... are called headers. There are two shops for the 'headers': one of these, where 48 children work, is 24 feet 9 inches by 20 feet, and 9 feet 1 inch high; it is lighted by two opposite rows of windows. This room is too small and too low for the numbers of workers and is very close at night, especially in the winter, when lights are required. For the use of 90 to 100 headers, boys and girls, there is one privy; this, at the period of my first visit, was loaded with excrement on the floor and elsewhere ...*
December 8th. All the children at work in both shops... the woman [in charge] was walking about with the cane in her hand, watching the children... Saw her through the window go and strike a child [children aged from 7-10]. 99 **(A)**

(*Parliamentary Papers,*Vol. *XIV,* 1843)

66 *1866. The boys were kept in constant motion [moving] throughout the day, each carrying from thirty to fifty dozen of moulds [from the potter's wheel] into the stoves [the kilns] and remaining long enough to take the dried earthenware away. The distance thus run by a boy in the course of a day...was estimated at seven miles. [The] children were rendered [made] pale, weak and unhealthy. In the depth of winter, with the thermometer in the open air sometimes below zero, boys, with little clothing but rags, might be seen running to and fro on errands*

or to their dinners with the perspiration [sweat] on their foreheads 'after labouring for hours like little slaves'. 99 **(B)**

(Eric Evans, *The Forging of the Modern State, 1783-1870,* 1983)

66 *Why did you leave off working at the cotton mills?*
I got tired of it, the system is so bad; and I had saved a few pounds. I got deformed there; my knees began to bend in when I was fifteen; you see how they are. [He is asked about accidents in cotton factories.] One girl, Mary Richards, was made a cripple, and remains so now, when I was in Lowdham mill near Nottingham; she was lapped up by a strap underneath the drawing frame.

Have you any children? Three.
Do you send them to factories?
No; I would rather have them transported. In the first place, they are standing upon one leg, lifting up one knee, a great part of the day, keeping the ends up from the spindle. I consider that that employment makes many cripples. Then there is the heat and the dust; then there are so many different forms of cruelty used upon them; then they are liable to have their fingers catched and to suffer other accidents from the machinery; then the hours is so long that I have seen them tumble down asleep among the straps and machinery, and so get cruelly hurt; then I would not have a child of mine there because there is not good morals; there is such a lot of them together that they learn mischief.

What are the forms of cruelty that you spoke of just now?
I have seen the time when two hand-vices of a pound weight each, more or less, have been screwed to my ears, at Lytton mill in Derbyshire. There are the scars still remaining behind my ears. 99 **(C)**

('Employment of Children in Manufactories', Second Report of the Central Board; *Parliamentary Papers,* Vol. *XXI,* 1833)

The country where this slavery existed is, of

course, Britain. Within the next 50 years Parliament passed the measures listed in factfile **F** to stamp out the abuse of child labour.

Young girls worked in the brickfields, carrying heavy loads of clay

F	**FACTFILE**

Factory reform, 1833-1878

Date	Event
1833	The 1833 **Factory Act** protects women and children in textile factories. Inspectors enforce the Act.
1842	**Mines Act.** Women and children under the age of 10 not to work underground. Mines inspectors appointed to enforce the measure.
1844	**Factory Act.** Children from 8-13 to work only 6½ hours before or after noon. 3 hours of schooling per day. Women and children from 13-18 can only work 12 hours a day.
1845	Women and children's night work in textile factories banned.
1847	**Ten Hours Bill.** Women and children can only work a 10-hour day in textile factories.
1867	**Factory Act.** Factory Acts cover all factories.
1874	**Factory Act.** Minimum age in textile factories raised to 9, (10 in 1875).
1875	Act passed to protect children working as chimney sweeps.
1878	**Factory and Workshops Act.** Women not to work more than 56½ hours a week in textile factories and 60 hours in other factories.

Matchbox makers at Bow, in London, 1871

Reporter!

To plan your TV programme, split the tasks up among you. Work on your own, in pairs, in groups or as a class.

1 Investigation (AT1, AT3)
• Mark out half the work area of the pin factory. If you can, arrange 24 chairs and desks in that space and see what it is like to work in.
• The noise in a cotton mill was so great that you could not be heard. Work out a way of talking or giving messages - remember that you cannot read or write.
• See how long you can spend standing on one leg, supporting yourself against a chair.
• Take the role of a child in **one** of the sources **A-E**. Study the source and note the facts about what your work would have been like. Think of things like noise, heat, smell, hunger, pain. On a sheet of paper, write down what a day in the factory is like and include **three** things that might have happened to you or your friends.

2 The enquiry (AT2, AT1)
Pass your accounts around and read them. Make a list of questions you would like to ask about factory life. In turn, class members have to answer questions about their lives (in-role). You can add to your sheet any new ideas you have.

3 The programme (AT1, AT2)
Design a headline for your story to show on screen, also captions and labels for any pictures you use, a cartoon to put your ideas across, and a date chart. Then work out how you will present: personal stories and interviews; a folk-song about working life; a detailed plan for laws to stop the abuses you have discovered; and a plan putting forward ideas for reform, see factfile **F**.

ACTIVITY · ACTIVITY ·

Mine Reform

Close your eyes. Think of keeping them closed for five minutes, 10 minutes, an hour, all day. How would you like it? Imagine travelling back 150 years in time. You could well have had to work in a mine. It would be pitch black below ground. If you worked a day shift you might only see the sun on a Sunday. In 1842 a government report laid bare what mine work meant for young people. I chose extracts **A-D** and pictures **E-G** from the report so that you could set up your own mining enquiry in your classroom.

The youngest children are entrusted with this important office! [Opening trap-doors to let in fresh air.] They are called trappers. Their duty consists in sitting in a little hole, scooped out for them in the side of the gates behind each door where they sit with a string in their hands attached to the door, and pull it the moment they hear the corves [wagons] at hand, and the moment it has passed they let the door fall to, which it does of its own weight... They are in the pit the whole time it is worked, frequently about 12 hours a day. They sit, moreover, in the dark, often with a damp floor to stand on... The age of these children varies from 5 to 10 years old... They are allowed no light but sometimes a good-natured collier will bestow a little bit of candle on them as a treat. **(A)**

Susan Pitchforth, aged 11... I have worked at this pit going two years. Come to work at eight or before, but I set off from home at seven. I walk a mile and half to my work, both in winter and summer. I get porridge for breakfast before I come, and bring my dinner with me - a muffin. When I have done about twelve loads I eat it while at work; I run 24 corves a day; I cannot come up till I have done them all. If I want to relieve myself I go into any part of the pit. [The commissioner] She stood shivering before me from cold. The rag that hung about her waist was once called a shift, which is as black as the coal she thrusts, and saturated with water from the dripping of the roof and shaft. **(B)**

I have to bear my burden up four traps, or ladders, before I get to the main road which leads to the pit bottom. My task is four or five tubs: each tub holds 4.25 cwt. I fill five tubs in twenty journeys... [H. Franks, an inspector] She takes the creel (a basket formed to the back, not unlike a cockle shell flattened towards the neck, so as to allow lumps of coal to rest on the back of the neck and shoulders). [She goes to the coal face.] She then lays down her basket, into which the coal is rolled, and it is frequently more than one man can do to lift the burden on her back. The tugs or straps are placed over the forehead, and the body bent in a semi-circular form, in order to stiffen the arch. **(C)**

I carry the large bits of coal from the wall-face to the pit bottom, and the small pieces called cows, in a creel; the weight is usually a hundredweight. The roof is very low; I have to bend my back and legs. [The pit is very wet.] **(D)**

(A-G are from the Parliamentary Commission's report on conditions in mines, *Parliamentary Papers*, Vol. XVI, 1842)

Women also dragged huge loads of coal along on sledges. In **1842** the **Mines Act** banned women and girls and boys under the age of 10 from working in mines, and appointed inspectors to make sure this happened.

F

G

Mine Enquiry

You can use the pictures and extracts to hold your own mine enquiry to get an idea of what working in a mine was like. The enquiry can take the form of a tape recording for your school library with a sheet of notes to go with it.

1 Thinking about the evidence (AT3)
The pictures.
• Split up **E-G** among you. Taking one picture, pick out **three** things you notice about it, work out what questions you would ask the worker(s), and decide on a single word or phrase which describes your feeling about the scene shown.
• Make out a class list of questions.
Written evidence.
• Read quickly through **A-D** and note down the ideas and thoughts the pieces give you.
• Read slowly through the pieces again, and list any words or phrases you do not know.
• In pairs, in groups or as a class, find out what these words or phrases mean.
• Choose one account from **A-D** and in 20 words sum up what it says.

2 Taking roles (AT1)
• Split into pairs. One of you is a mining inspector, the other imagines that he or she is **one** of the people shown in **each** of the different pictures.
• From **E-G** note down what the pictures suggest about your life.
• Then the inspector asks you questions worked out in part **1**.
• Write down the answers. Each group can report back on what it has found out about mine work.
• Say what it might be like to be someone of your age: going down the mine; working as a trapper, or dragging a sledge with a chain, or pulling a wagon, or carrying a creel; involved in an explosion and fire in the pit.

3 Reform (AT2)
Draw up a plan for mine reform from the point of view of **either** a rich mine owner **or** a fierce enemy of child labour and women working in mines.

57

Crime and Punishment

A

Today if your best friend was murdered, who would you ask to solve the crime? In 1750 who might have helped? It could have depended on where you lived. In most areas of England the poorly paid parish constable and night watchman tried to keep the law, but London had a tiny body of police, the Bow Street Runners. In 1829, in London, Sir Robert Peel set up the first modern police force, the Metropolitan Police. Do you know what nickname for policemen, **A**, comes from Peel's name? A law passed in 1835 said that all towns could set up such police forces - a measure that spread to the counties in 1839. In 1856 the County Police Act forced **all** counties to have a police force.

Before 1826 you could be hanged for over 100 crimes, ranging from stealing a sheep to damaging Westminster Bridge. In 1826 Peel swept away these old laws and put in their place a much simpler, clearer and fairer code. Punishments stayed the same for most crimes, so you could still be transported [sent] to Australia for seven years for what we would now think was a petty crime. **B** and **C** are taken from court cases in Shropshire between 1820 and 1830.

April 1830. John Haughton, aged 29, was convicted of having stolen 83 iron tram-rails, the property of the Lilleshall Company, from the mouth of a coal-pit at Wrockardine Wood, and was sentenced to be imprisoned to hard labour for 6 calendar months.

Thomas Salt and Thomas Nevett were convicted of having stolen 3cwt of Hay, the property of Mr Henry Skelding of Bridgnorth. Salt had been previously twice convicted of felony, and he was therefore now sentenced to be transported for 7 years, and Nevett was sentenced to be imprisoned for three calendar months.

Allen Pinches (an old offender) was convicted of having stolen a pair of shoes, the property of Mr John Roden of Shiffnal, innkeeper, and was sentenced to be imprisoned to 6 months' hard labour. **(B)**

(*The Salopian Journal* - the local newspaper)

The court record for the case of the stolen hay reads:

George Southwell of Bridgnorth, carpet weaver, was near the bridge and passing by the side of the river up Shut Lane towards the New Factory. About 100 yards from the bridge a person with a truss of hay on his back passed him. In Shut Lane he was passed by Thos Nevett with a truss of hay on his back. Southwell overtook Nevett at the top of the lane and Nevett threw down the hay which Southwell told him he had stole. Next morning he saw Nevett at the Bull Inn and charged him. Nevett took him by the shoulder and said, "Damn you, if I had seen you in such a job I would never have split on you." **(C)**

(Quarter Session records, Shropshire)

Prison reform went hand in hand with changes in the law and policing. From 1791 each county could build its own gaol - before this there had been hundreds of local lock-ups. The work of reformers, such as Elizabeth Fry and John Howard, led Peel to extend government control over prisons in 1823. Magistrates now inspected them - before this there had been no control over them.

In 1853 transportation ended, so the Government had to build new, long-stay prisons - like the prisons we have today, such as Dartmoor and Brixton. Prison life was harsh. Prisoners had to work for hours each day on the treadmill, **D**, or use a hand mill to grind corn. In some prisons - penitentiaries - you were locked up all day by yourself and not allowed to talk to or see anyone. You spent all your time praying and reading the Bible. What do you think lay behind this reform?

Crime File!

Plan and prepare items for a talk to eight-year-olds on crime and punishment from 1830 to 1860, noting how things had changed since 1750. Use sources **A-C** as a guide. You can split the tasks up among you.

1 Research (AT3)
• Who might have acted as your local policeman in 1750, 1830 and 1860?
• Why were policemen dressed as in picture **A**, and how does this compare with a modern policeman's uniform?
• How might your local prisons have changed from 1750 to 1830?
• What defence might Thomas Nevett have had when charged with stealing hay?
• What evidence is there that he was guilty?
• Note three things about working on a treadmill, **D**. Pool your ideas.
• Find out about Elizabeth Fry, John Howard, Peel's reforms, penitentiaries.

2 Crime table (AT1)
Make out a list of crimes that you know about today. Then set up a court to try them as if it was 1830. Decide on the punishment you would inflict, choosing from: whipping; prison; prison with hard labour - one month, three months, six months; transportation; hanging.

Make out a table with the following headings:

Crime	Punishment today	Punishment in 1830

3 Prison visit (AT1)
If you visited the criminals you jailed in 1830, say what the jail might have been like and what work the prisoners did. Write your story as an interview with one of the prisoners in **B**, at work on **D**. Brainstorm ideas and key words with others.

4
You can present your ideas to your class, and then choose the items you want to include in your school talk.

Public Health

A Third World country? The journalist is writing a story about life in the slums of the country's main port. Dr Duncan is his guide. The city council has built sewers for the upper class, but the doctor says:

> *With regard to the streets inhabited by the working classes, I believe that the great majority are without sewers, and that where they do exist they are of a very imperfect kind unless where the ground has a natural inclination [slope] therefore the surface water and fluid refuse of every kind stagnate in the street, and add, especially in hot weather, their pestilential influence [disease] to that of the more solid filth already mentioned. With regard to the courtyards, I doubt whether there is a single court…which communicates with the street by an underground drain, the only means for…carrying off the fluid dirt being a narrow, open, shallow gutter which sometimes exists, but even this is very generally choked up with stagnant filth.* **(A)**

Dr Duncan then says that he is sure that the sewage causes disease. To back up his views he talks of his visit to one courtyard:

> *63 cases of fever had occurred in one year at Union Court, Banastre Street, containing 12 houses. I visited the court in order to find out, if possible, their origin. I found the whole court flooded with fluid filth which had oozed through the walls from two adjoining ash-pits or cess-pools, and which had no means of escape because the court was below the level of the street and had no drain.* **(B)**

Most of the city's houses have no running water or flushing toilets. The journalist then goes to the capital city and visits an area like **C**, in which disease kills many of the working class. Table **D** shows who died in a year out of 62,000 people living in one part of the capital:

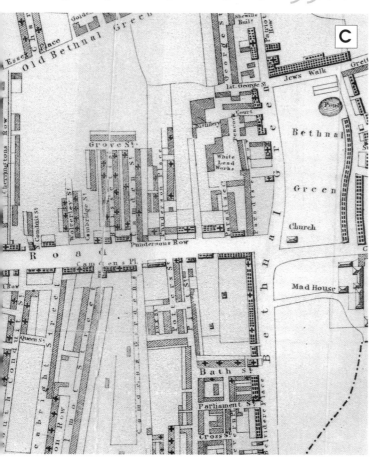

D		
No. of deaths	**Class**	**Average age at death**
101	Gentlemen and persons engaged in professions and their families	45 years
273	Tradesmen and their families	26 years
1,248	Craftsmen, servants and labourers and their families	16 years

I found picture **E** of a street in the capital. **E** ties in with sources **A-D**.

Have you guessed which country sources **A-E** are from? The answer is Britain, and **A-D** are from a report written in 1842 about the state of Britain's towns and cities. Before 1842 each town and city was in charge of its own drainage, paving, lighting and refuse collection. Disease and death were so widespread that the Government decided to act - see factfile **F**.

Do you think this is a real street or a made-up one?

FACTFILE

F

Date	Event
1801-50	Towns and cities were growing by 25% every 10 years. Working-class areas grew up in town centres. Back-to-back housing was common. The middle classes moved to the suburbs.
1830-32	Cholera killed over 30,000 people in towns and cities.
1842	Edwin Chadwick published his **Sanitary Report** (sources **A-D**).
1848	**Public Health Act.** Towns could set up a Local Health Board to build and maintain drains, sewers and toilets; supply fresh water; pave and clean the streets; inspect lodging houses and shops and businesses; and run burial grounds.
1855	About **300 towns** had set up Local Health Boards. Government Board of Health brought about major changes in public health.
1866	**Sanitary Act.** Towns had to have sanitary inspectors who made sure the towns were kept in a healthy state.
1872-75	**Public Health Acts** - Country split up into sanitary authorities, with medical officers and sanitary inspectors. - Local authorities had to lay sewers, drains and pavements and keep streets clean and well lit. - Local authorities had to deal with diseases and epidemics.
1875	**Artisans' Dwellings Act.** Councils were able to clear slum districts.

Health Planner

How good a health planner might you have been for area **C** or for your local area in the 1850s? If the Local Health Board had asked you to draw up a public health plan in 1850, what would you have done? Work on your own, in pairs or in groups.

1 The problem (AT3)
Use **A-E** to list the things that you have to put right. For your own area, try and find out what it was like before the Public Health Act of 1848.

2 The features (AT3)
Use an enlarged map of **C** or a map of your own area and work out where the following should go:

a water works; a main water pipe, with side pipes to all streets; a main sewer, with drains and sewers running from side streets into it; a public toilet in each side road; paving for all streets.

3 The plan (AT1)
Draw up a plan for the area, saying how you would keep the streets clean, inspect lodging houses, shops and businesses, and make sure the burial grounds were well run.

4 The Local Health Board (AT1)
The class can take the role of the Local Health Board, and judge which is the best plan.

Trade Unions

What is a trade union? When were the first ones set up? What did they do? I love old trade union membership cards like **A**. It tells you what the union tried to do for its members. Before 1824 it was against the law to belong to such a union. Workers fought fierce battles to set up unions, such as **A**, to help both men and women who slaved away in factories like **B**. The history of trade unions goes through four periods - **1793-1824, 1825-35, 1836-70** and **1871-1900**, see factfile **C**. It was not until the 1880s and 1890s that trade unions had the powers to look after women and unskilled workers.

A

Membership certificate of the ASCJ

Trade Union!

Split into four groups. Each group chooses **one** of the four periods in factfile **C** in which to set up a trade union. It can be for workers in the envelope factory on page 31, the workers in **B**, or for pupils in your school.

1 The rules (AT1, AT3)
The union will have to obey the law or become a secret society. Using **C** and anything else you can find out, decide:
• What working conditions are like now: pay, hours, conditions, workers' rights, what happens to injured or sick workers.
• What kind of union it will be - ie. a friendly society, a craft union, a new model union.
• What the aims of the union are.
• What it will cost to join.
• What its rules are.
• How it will fight for its members' rights in factories like **B**. Think of: hours, wages, conditions, holidays, sick pay.
• Will it join with other unions to form a national body?

2 The membership card, banner and song (AT3, AT2)
• Work out from **A** the things a membership card should have on it.
• Use the rules of your union in designing your own membership card or trade union banner **or** make up a trade union song about your union.
• Display your cards and banners and sing your songs.

3 Strike! (AT2)
You decide to hold a strike. Think about what you would do and about what might happen. Talk about it among yourselves. In turn, answer questions about the strike from members of a government enquiry.

ACTIVITY · ACTIVITY

Women workers in a cycle factory, 1897

FACTFILE

C

Date	Event	Date	Event
1750-1800	End of the old guild system in new factory towns. Workers began to set up **friendly societies** instead to protect themselves.		Society of Engineers (ASE). Union opposed to strikes, used its money to help its sick and out-of-work members and to pay pensions. Spread of model unions to most other groups of skilled workers.
1793	**Friendly Societies Act** protects their funds.		
1793+	The fear of French Revolutionary ideas spreading to England in 1799-1800 led to the **Combination Acts** which banned all trade unions.	1868	**Trades Union Congress** founded for all unions. Each year all the unions meet to protect their joint interests.
1811-12	Luddite riots, see page 48.	1870s	Unions set up to protect **unskilled** workers in industries such as coal mining and farming.
1824	**Combination Acts repealed**. Outbreak of hundreds of strikes.	1888	**Annie Besant** led match making girls in a strike against long hours and dangerous working conditions at Bryant & May's match factory. Making matches could cause the girls' jaws to rot away - a disease called 'phossy jaw'. The match girls gained huge public support and won.
1825	Government passed an **act to ban strikes**.		
1829-34	Failure of the attempt to set up a **national trade union** for cotton workers.		
1834	**Tolpuddle Martyrs**. Six Dorset farm labourers arrested for trying to form a trade union by taking secret oaths. They were deported to Australia. Huge outcry against their treatment. They are still a symbol of worker persecution.	1889	Major **dock strike** for pay of 6d (2.5p) an hour and a change in the way that casual dock workers were hired and fired. The dockers won their 'docker's tanner'. Mass unions now fully accepted and legal.
1851	First new **model union** set up for skilled workers - Amalgamated		

Education

'Crisis in Education - read all about it!' the newspaper seller might have shouted in 1870 as well as today. Nothing changes, for in 1870 the Government was so worried about the state of British education that it rushed through a major Education Act. Why? There were three main reasons or **causes**:

1 The German army of well-schooled soldiers had just routed the French army of soldiers, most of whom could not read or write. It seemed that literate soldiers fought better. Why?
2 German industry was becoming a major threat to British industry. Educated German workers worked better than the poorly educated British. Can you think why?
3 British working-class men had been given the vote in 1867. Who might illiterate voters choose as their MPs and why do you think this was feared?

Before 1870 children were taught either in a factory, in a workhouse (see page 52), in church schools or privately. Most children went to church schools until they were 10 years old. There were two kinds, those run by the Church of England (C. of E.) and those in the hands of non-conformist churches such as the Baptists and Methodists, see pages 66-68. The C. of E. and the nonconformists fought like cats and dogs over who should have charge of education - can you say why? Today you may well go to a church school - how does this affect what you learn? Although schools were common in 1870, one third of all children had no schooling at all.

The Government would help pay for schools if they were inspected and if the children reached a certain standard in reading, writing and arithmetic - the three Rs, **A**. This system was called **payment by results**. Teachers hated it - what impact might it have had on their teaching? In 1870 the Government's Act aimed to provide schooling for **ALL** children. It set up local school boards to run the new state schools. In 1880 all children had to go to an elementary school until the age of 10. In 1891 schooling became free - before then you'd had to pay.

What was school life like? **B** is a normal school day's timetable. **C** was used for handwriting practice while **D** is a lesson plan for teaching about the turnip. **E** gives an idea of what school was like.

The whole school assembles in the morning in the central hall... After saluting the headmaster and teachers a hymn is sung, some simple prayers are said, and then the children go to their class rooms for half an hour's Religious Education based on selected parts of the Bible. **(E)**

(A school inspector's report from the 1880s)

The three educational standards of the 'payment by results' system			
	Standard I	**Standard II**	**Standard III**
Reading	Narrative in monosyllables	One of the narratives next in order after monosyllables in an elementary reading book used in the school	A short paragraph from an elementary reading book used in the school
Writing	Form on blackboard or slate from dictation letters capital and small manuscript	Copy in manuscript character a line of print	A sentence from the same paragraph slowly read once, and then dictated in single words
Arithmetic	Form on blackboard or slate from dictation figures up to 20; name at sight figures up to 20; add and subtract figures up to 10	A sum in simple addition and subtraction, and the multiplication table	A sum in simple rule as far as short division **A**

B

A school day - Standard III, 1889

9.00- 9.05	Examine cleanliness	
9.05- 9.20	Scripture	
9.20- 9.30	Mental arithmetic	
9.30- 9.40	Registration	
9.40-10.30	Arithmetic	
10.30-11.10	Spelling and dictation	
11.10-11.20	Singing	
11.20-12.00	Reading	
2.00- 2.10	Registration	
	Boys	**Girls**
2.10- 3.10	Drawing	Needlework
3.10- 3.50	History	History
3.50- 4.30	Reading	Reading

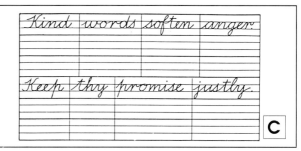

(Jo Lawrie and Paul Noble, *Victorian Times*)

TURNIPS.　　D

APPARATUS.—A turnip (the whole plant), or sketch of same, several varieties of turnips, a few carrots, parsnips, radishes; turnip seed.

AIM.—To show the growth, composition, and uses of the turnip; and to contrast, in these points, with other vegetables.

I. Introduction.—Children are always ready for dinner when they reach home at noon. Often first question is, 'What is there for dinner, mother?' Some do not care for meat—nearly all like—what? Potatoes.

[Then elicit what other **vegetables** they like until **turnips** are named.]

II. Where and how Turnips grow.—(Town children perhaps never saw them growing — very familiar to country children.) Where do they grow? In gardens and fields. Here is one just taken out of a garden.

[Note shape, colour, leaves.]

How is it we do not see the turnips growing? Grow underground. (Other vegetables that do—none exactly like turnip—potato and carrot quite different in shape and colour.) The turnip is not an *ordinary* root, but a kind of *storehouse of food* for the growth of the plant next year.

[Note **little roots** growing out of the thick fleshy roots of turnips and carrots.]

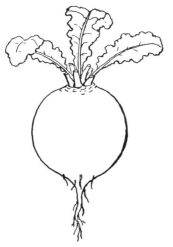

A Turnip.

How do we know when the turnips are ripe, if we cannot see them growing? They peep out from the ground as if saying, 'I'm quite ready for eating.'

[Draw attention to the *white* part which was underground and the *coloured* part above, and explain why this difference in colour.]

Potatoes never peep above ground—too deep down and fast on the bunch of stringy stems from which they grow. Turnips grow from seeds.

(*Chambers's Object Lesson Manuals*, 1897)

School Inspection - Logbook

At various times a government inspector would have visited your school. The school logbook would have recorded what went on. Using our sources we can re-create such an inspection for 11 December 1899, which you can perform for a class or a whole-school assembly.

1 Getting ready (AT3, AT1)
You can get your lessons ready for the inspection at Standard III for 10-year-olds in Dictation, Reading, Writing, an Object Lesson and History:

Dictation Write out a sentence that your teacher dictates.

Reading In turns, you will be asked to read a paragraph from a school reading book.

Writing On lined or ruled paper, copy the words in **C** as shown.

Object Lesson Answer the questions in **D** for a carrot instead of a turnip.

History
• List the types of school in Britain before 1900.
• Give three reasons for the 1870 Education Act.
• When did state education become compulsory in Britain? Until what age?
• What was a standard?
• What was payment by results?
• Which Act was passed in 1867 and with what result?
The lesson will take place in complete silence.

2 The logbook (AT2, AT1)
Write a logbook entry for the visit of the school inspector. Say how the lessons went and how many pupils reached Standard III.

3 Then and now (AT1)
Make out a timetable comparing a day in your school life with that of a pupil in 1900.

Methodism

Pop into your local church and try to work out how people pray in it. Where is the altar? Is there a pulpit, and if so, how important is it? Does the church have lots of statues, pictures and stained glass? Is it painted in bright colours or is it plain white? What faith is it?

In England there are many types of Christianity, including Roman Catholicism, the Church of England and Methodism. The newest of these is Methodism. The founder of Methodism was John Wesley (1703-1791). To help you work out for yourselves what Methodism meant, I used some of my books to write factfile **B** and to pick out sources **A** and **C-F**. Try and visit a Methodist church to see how the ideas on this page tie in with how you think the building is used to pray to God.

Historians think Methodism appealed to people for many reasons. Wesley said that those who prayed to God and studied the Bible would go to heaven. He won many converts. The Church of England had few followers among the working class in the new industrial towns and cities of the Midlands and the North and growing ports like Hull and Bristol. Methodism appealed strongly to workers who were looking for a meaning to life. Wesley's preaching about God gave it to them.

It had never occurred to him to preach anywhere but inside a church until he received an invitation to preach in the open air at Bristol. The request came from George Whitefield (1714-1770), a well-known preacher who was working among the coal miners of Kingswood, a village some four miles from the city, beyond the reach of any parish church. Whitefield preached to them in the open air and with great success, but he had to leave for America and wanted Wesley to continue his work. Wesley was doubtful. This was against all church traditions and having gone to Bristol he wrote in his Journal (April 1st 1739): "I could scarce reconcile myself at first to this strange way of preaching of which he [Mr Whitefield] set me an example on Sunday." *Yet he wrote again on the Monday: "At four in the afternoon I submitted to be more vile and proclaimed in the highways the glad tidings of salvation, speaking from a little eminence [hill] in a ground adjoining to the city to about 30,000 people."*

So Wesley began a method of preaching that he kept up for the rest of his life. In market places, church-yards, in streets and on open moors he gathered crowds, sometimes in thousands... It is reckoned that Wesley travelled a quarter of a million miles, mostly on horseback, in the fifty or so years of his preaching tours. **(A)**

(Jim Bates, *The Methodist Church*, 1977)

FACTFILE

B	
Date	**Event**
1738	Wesley, a Church of England priest, converted to evangelicalism.
1739	Began open-air preaching and decided to build the first Methodist meeting house at Bristol.
1740	Used preachers who were not Church of England priests.
1742	The first setting up of the Methodist 'class system' - meetings broke into groups of twelve members, each with a leader.
1744	First annual conference of Methodist preachers.
1740s+	Wesley spread the word on his preaching tours and built up a large following in the ports and new industrial areas of England.
1791	Wesley died - having founded 2,000 societies with around 85,000 members.
1800-50	Rapid growth of Methodism.
1990	10,000 Methodist societies in existence.

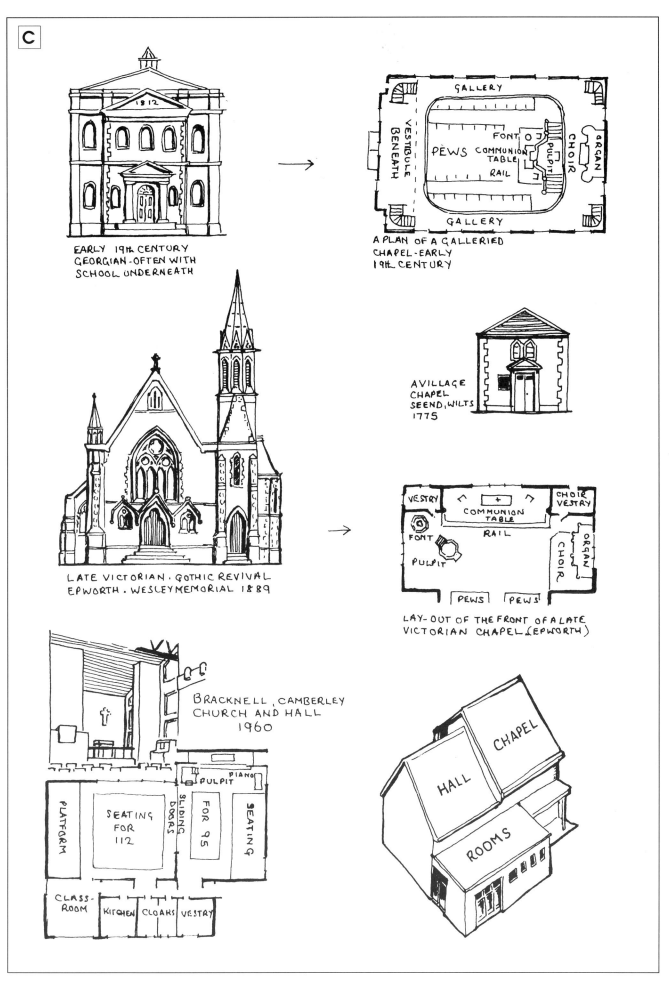

C

EARLY 19th CENTURY
GEORGIAN·OFTEN WITH
SCHOOL UNDERNEATH

A PLAN OF A GALLERIED
CHAPEL·EARLY
19th CENTURY

LATE VICTORIAN·GOTHIC REVIVAL
EPWORTH·WESLEY MEMORIAL 1889

A VILLAGE
CHAPEL
SEEND, WILTS
1775

LAY-OUT OF THE FRONT OF A LATE
VICTORIAN CHAPEL (EPWORTH)

BRACKNELL, CAMBERLEY
CHURCH AND HALL
1960

Plans of Methodist churches

> 66 *Come, Holy Ghost, all-quickening fire,*
> *Come and in me delight to rest,*
> *Drawn by the lure of strong desire,*
> *O come and consecrate my breast.* 99 **(D)**
>
> (A Methodist hymn)

The first Methodist conference, 1744

Methodism!

You can try and create in your classroom an idea of what Methodism meant for people in the eighteenth century. Finding out can be a class quiz for two teams. You can work on the tasks in point **2** as a class.

1 Finding out (AT3)
Use **A-F** and any other sources you can find to answer these questions:
• What did Wesley learn from Whitefield?
• When did Wesley start to preach in this way, and why?
• Where did he preach, and to whom?
• How far did he travel, and for how long?
• What was a meeting?
• What was the class system?
• What was the annual conference?
• When Wesley died, how many Methodists were there?
• How many societies were there?
• How many societies are there today?
• What message does **D** contain?

• What do all the church plans have in common?
• What message does **F** send about how Wesley ran the Methodist Movement?
• When did Methodism grow quickly?

2 Methodism in action (AT1, AT2)
• **Plan out** your classroom as a Methodist meeting room. Base it on the ideas in **C**, with the main focus being the preacher. Make sure that all the congregation can see the preacher, leave space for people to gather for communion, and provide seating for the choir and a place for an organ or piano.
• Write a prayer for a Methodist service for 10-year-old children.
• Choose a reading from the Bible for them.
• Design a preaching cloak and shirt front for a preacher similar to the ones that Wesley used, **E** and **F**.
• Write a hymn, like **D**, for a Methodist meeting.

Church Reform

A

St Dyfnog's Church, Llanrhaeadr, restored 1879-1880

The Church of England was a shambles in 1832. Far too many priests did not live in their parishes and spent their time hunting, fishing, shooting and enjoying themselves.

In the 1830s and 1840s a wind of change swept through the Church of England to meet the threat from Methodism and make sure that the new industrial areas of England had enough C. of E. (Anglican) churches and priests. From 1831 to 1851 the number of Anglican churches in Lancashire increased from 292 to 521. The same thing was happening in every urban area - church growth was even quicker than population growth!

You are fairly certain to have one of these new churches near to where you live or, if your local church is an old one, you will find that the Victorians ripped out its insides and completely rebuilt it. **A** is a typical nineteenth-century Anglican church - I picked it because my wife's grandfather was the vicar there!

In the Church of England the Oxford Movement had a huge influence. Its leaders claimed that the C. of E. should go back to the forms of worship it had followed in Tudor times. These were very like Roman Catholicism - lots of chanting, ritual and rich ornament. In the nineteenth century most people believed in God and went to church. The Church played a huge part in everyone's lives, as there was then no Welfare State to look after you. Your local vicar looked after you instead!

Church Reform!

You can try and puzzle out what a reformed Church of England might have done in your own area in the 1850s. Work through the following points:

1 The school hall (AT3, AT2)
Your school hall is going to be rebuilt as an Anglican chapel. Draw up plans along the lines of **A**. Look at the pews, windows, walls, altar and floor. Compare your plans with those for Methodist churches on page 67.

2 The vicar (AT2)
You have to appoint a vicar to look after the chapel and the people who live around it. Make out a job advert, saying what kind of person you want and what that person will have to do. Think about:
- organising church services
- looking after the church
- caring for the poor
- teaching
- the kind of person you want.

ACTIVITY · ACTIVITY ·

Trade and Empire

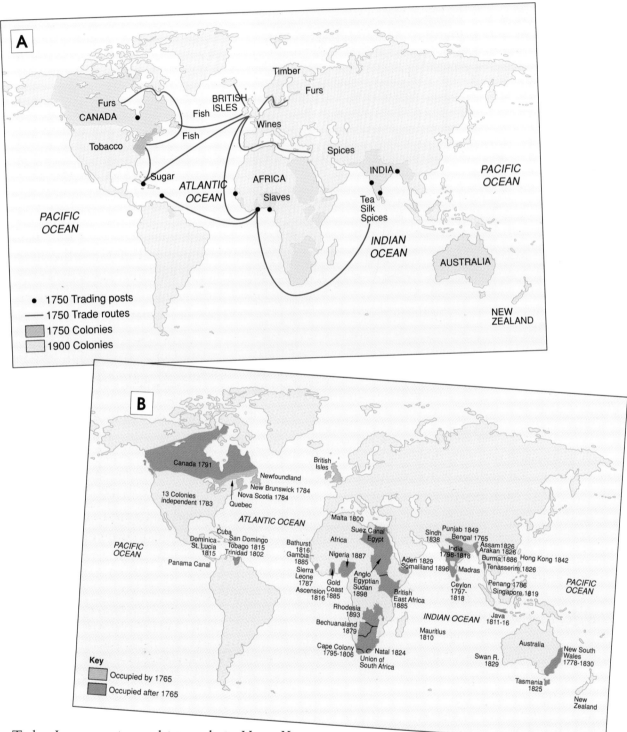

A

Timber
Furs
Furs
BRITISH ISLES
CANADA
Fish
Wines
Fish
Tobacco
Spices
INDIA
Sugar
ATLANTIC OCEAN
AFRICA
PACIFIC OCEAN
Slaves
Tea
Silk
Spices
PACIFIC OCEAN
INDIAN OCEAN
AUSTRALIA
NEW ZEALAND

- 1750 Trading posts
— 1750 Trade routes
■ 1750 Colonies
□ 1900 Colonies

B

Canada 1791
British Isles
Newfoundland
New Brunswick 1784
Nova Scotia 1784
13 Colonies independent 1783
Quebec
ATLANTIC OCEAN
Malta 1800
Suez Canal
Sindh 1838
Punjab 1849
Bengal 1765
PACIFIC OCEAN
Cuba
Dominica
St. Lucia 1815
San Domingo
Tobago 1815
Trinidad 1802
Bathurst 1816
Gambia 1885
Africa
Egypt
India 1798-1818
Assam 1826
Arakan 1826
Burma 1886
Hong Kong 1842
Panama Canal
Nigeria 1887
Aden 1829
Somaliland 1896
Madras
Tenasserim 1826
Sierra Leone 1787
Ascension 1816
Gold Coast 1885
Anglo Egyptian Sudan 1898
British East Africa 1885
Ceylon 1797-1818
Penang 1786
Singapore 1819
PACIFIC OCEAN
Rhodesia 1893
Bechuanaland 1879
INDIAN OCEAN
Java 1811-16
Mauritius 1810
Australia
Cape Colony 1795-1806
Natal 1824
Union of South Africa
Swan R. 1829
New South Wales 1778-1830
Tasmania 1825
New Zealand

Key
■ Occupied by 1765
■ Occupied after 1765

Today I am wearing a shirt made in Hong Kong. For lunch I will have New Zealand lamb and some Canadian cheese, washed down with a bottle of Australian wine. Tonight we will go out to an Indian restaurant for a curry.

All around you there are clues which tell you that Britain built up a huge empire after 1750 - street names, foods, clothes, and people who used to live in Britain's colonies. Over the past 100 years, how many members of your family have gone to live abroad? Where and why? How many members of your family have come to live in Britain from the old colonies? The British Empire still has an impact on our lives.

In 1750 the British Empire was tiny - a handful of American colonies and trading posts in Africa and India, **A**. Expanding trade between England, Africa, America and the West Indies, see pages 74-75, meant that ports like Liverpool and Bristol mushroomed. After 1780 Britain lost its American colonies, pages 76-77, but built up a huge new empire based on **India**. This empire grew quickly from 1750 to 1830, pages 78-79. British rule in India and booming trade in the Far East led to the setting up of new colonies in Asia, such as Singapore and Hong Kong.

From 1830 onwards Britain gained many new colonies around the world, **B**, often to protect her traders, **C**. Some historians have called this the **Imperialism of Free Trade**. After 1870 the British Empire took on its final form when Britain took part in the **Scramble for Africa**, see pages 80-81.

Here are some reasons why the British gained an empire:

1 **Technology**   European forces used modern guns and ships to defeat poorly-armed native armies.

2 **Training of troops**   European armies were well trained and highly disciplined - usually those of the natives were not.

3 **Industry**   Britain had large amounts of goods to sell abroad and needed raw materials for its factories.

4 **Local trade**   British traders needed Britain to take over a region for them to trade in.

5 **European rivalry**   Britain often seized colonies because it was afraid that other countries might do so instead.

6 **Investment**   The money made from the Industrial Revolution was invested in colonies.

7 **Settlement**   British people wanting to live abroad needed colonies to live in.

8 **Local causes**   The British who were trading or in charge of armed forces in an area often took over a colony in Britain's name without asking the Government at home.

9 **The Indian route**   Britain took over some countries to protect the British route to India.

10 **Combined**   A number of the reasons above.

C	Liverpool trade in 1900											
Place	**Goods imported into UK**											
	a	b	c	d	e	f	g	h	i	j	k	l
America	x	x	x	x		x						
Argentina				x		x						
Australia		x			x	x						
Balkans	x											
Brazil							x					
Canada						x						
Egypt			x									
Europe											x	
Greece										x		
India								x	x			
New Zealand					x							
Peru												x
Russia	x											
S Africa						x		x				

Key **a** grain **b** gold **c** cotton **d** meat **e** wool **f** wheat **g** fruit **h** tea **i** rice **j** grapes, currants **k** machinery **l** *guano* [bird droppings]

The History Archive

Create a history archive on trade and empire.

1 History archive - finding out about the British Empire (AT3)
• As a class, work out how many of your relatives and ancestors either came from, or have gone to live in, any of the countries on **B**.
• If you can, interview someone you know who has lived in any of the countries shown and present his or her story to the class.
• List all the goods you can buy from these countries. Use labels, adverts and posters to make a class display about them.
• Think of street names, shops, restaurants and pubs that tell us about the British Empire.
• What aspects of popular music, art and sport can you link to the colonies in **B**?
• Find out how Britain gained one of its colonies, and then see which of the reasons you have discovered match those in the text.

2 Trade (AT1)
Use map **B** to work out when you could first trade in the goods shown in **C** and the goods you found out about in part **1** above.

Black Hole of Calcutta

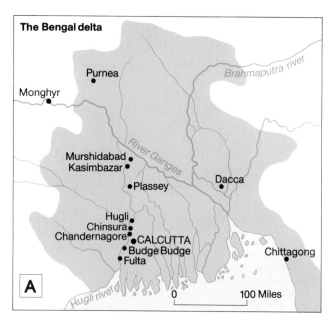

The Bengal delta

A

so great you can form no idea. This brought on a raging thirst which grew greater as the body was drained of moisture. Various things we thought of to give more room and air. To obtain the former it was moved to put off their clothes. This was approved as a happy idea, and in a few minutes I believe every man was stripped... Every hat was put in motion to produce a movement of air. 🙶 **(B)**

(J.Z. Holwell, *Memoirs*, 1758)

When the guards opened the door in the morning a handful of men stumbled out alive. A pile of bodies lay on the floor of the Black Hole. A horror story had been born.

1756. Siraj ud Daulah, the new young ruler of Bengal, was furious. The British had failed to pay the money he had demanded from them. As one of Bengal's richest group of traders, the British could afford it. He would teach them a lesson. In the past the old ruler, his grandfather, had marched his army down to the gates of the main British trading city, Calcutta, see **A**, to squeeze money out of the British. He would do the same. Siraj's huge force of 50,000 men and elephants lumbered towards Calcutta. Still the British would not pay. So in July Siraj's army stormed the city. Many of the British fled down the river in their boats; those remaining were made prisoners of Siraj. One of them, John Zephaniah Holwell, takes up the story of how they were forced into the local gaol, the Black Hole:

🙶 *Figure to yourself, the state of 146 wretches, worn out by non stop fatigue and activity, thus crammed together in a cube of about eighteen feet. A close, sultry night in Bengal. We were shut up to the east and south (the only quarters from which air could reach us) by dead walls, and by a wall and door to the north, open only to the west by two windows, strongly barred wih iron, from which we could scarce receive the least breath of fresh air. We had been but a few minutes shut up before everyone fell into a sweat*

Front Page

Produce a front page for a history newspaper from the point of view of **either** an **Indian** backer of Siraj **or** the **British.** Work on your own, in pairs, or in teams of three to four.

1 The attack and what happened (AT3, AT2)
• Work out why Siraj attacked the British and what happened when he entered Calcutta and put the British into the Black Hole.
• Brainstorm a list of words that describe what it was like in the Black Hole when the British went in - at midnight and in the morning.
• Mime the scene.
• How true is the story of the Black Hole? Only Holwell wrote about it at the time; there is no way of checking if the story is true. (He was a famous liar!)

2 Front page (AT2)
Produce: a headline; the first paragraph of a news report on the Black Hole; a plan of the prison; an account of what went on in the form of interviews with the guards and survivors; a drawing and a cartoon of what it was like in the Black Hole. Then use points 1-9 on page 71 to say how the British might try to win back Calcutta.

ACTIVITY · ACTIVITY

Plassey

At Madras, in the south of India, Britain had a small fleet and army to fight her bitter enemies, the French. On hearing the news of Calcutta's fall, this force rushed north, won back Calcutta and marched towards Siraj's capital. At Siraj's court Robert Clive, the commander of the British army, began to plot with Siraj's army commanders, bankers and merchants to overthrow Siraj. The capture of Calcutta by Siraj had wrecked the fortunes of these bankers and merchants. Before 1756 they had traded with the British, but now all trade had stopped. The overthrow of Siraj might repair their fortunes, as trade would get back to normal. The merchants, generals and Clive wrote to each other in code, **A**. Mir Jafir was the general in charge of Siraj's troops.

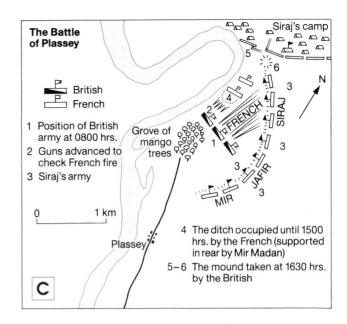

The Battle of Plassey

- British
- French
1 Position of British army at 0800 hrs.
2 Guns advanced to check French fire
3 Siraj's army
4 The ditch occupied until 1500 hrs. by the French (supported in rear by Mir Madan)
5-6 The mound taken at 1630 hrs. by the British

0   1 km

C

A	*Clive to Mir Jafir, 17 June 1757*

3839 38 2920424 C'3831 19342926
22181924 25193424 2238164 262335
192724 21 182322 1929 38 2423 192724?
2339 19164 241838322831 24193320
27193420 2339 2623353431201639 24181924
262335 1520 322324 353230233220 1526
243420192718203426 152039233420 2926
1934438131916

Code C' = *th*; 1 =. (*full stop*); 4 = *repeat previous letter*;
13 = *v*; 14 = *j*; 15 = *b*; 16 = *l*; 17 = *x*; 18 = *h*; 19 = *a*;
20 = *e*; 21 = *and*; 22 = *w*; 23 = *o*; 24 = *t*; 25 = *p*; 26= *y*;
27 = *c*; 28 = *g*; 29 = *m*; 30 = *d*; 31 = *s*; 32 = *n*; 33 = *k*;
34 = *r*; 35 = *u*; 36 = *z*; 37 = *q*; 38 = *i*; 39 = *f*.

B	Clive's army	Siraj's army
	2,100 trained Indian soldiers	35,000 footsoldiers
	850 European footsoldiers	15, 000 cavalry
	150 artillerymen	500 artillerymen
	8 quick-firing six-pound guns	53 slow-firing
	1 howitzer	cannon

The two sides were not matched for size or for guns, **B**. On the morning of 23 June the two armies drew up to fight. A small French force helped Siraj. The French, Siraj and Mir Jafir penned in the British, **C**. Siraj's troops pushed forward. Clive's guns peppered Siraj's elephants, who turned and rushed through the ranks of Siraj's army crushing everyone in their way. Panic broke out and Siraj's forces fled. Mir Jafir failed to fight for Siraj - treachery! The battle was soon over. Clive made Mir Jafir the new ruler of Bengal. Mir Jafir gave Clive £250,000 as a reward. Within 10 years the British had taken over Bengal's government. Bengal was India's richest province, so the base for Britain's Indian empire was secure.

Plassey - Encyclopedia

In 100 words write your own account of the battle, based on your work in points **1-3** below, for a children's encyclopedia.

1 Researching the background (AT3)
- On graph paper plot the size of the two armies (50 soldiers to each square).
- Work out two reasons why Clive might win the battle, and two reasons why he might lose. Agree on a list of reasons with a partner.
- Work out the meaning of **A**.

2 Spy messages (AT2, AT1)
Write a message in code: Clive to Mir Jafir, as Siraj's army gets ready to attack.

3 Points of view (AT2, AT1)
Write three sentences on the battle from the viewpoint of: Clive; Mir Jafir; Siraj.

The Slave Trade

Have you ever wondered what we mean when we say someone 'slaves away'? Between 1600 and 1850, millions of Africans were made slaves and sent to America. Slaves might have been prisoners of war, debtors or criminals. How did the slave trade work? To show you I picked out extracts **A**, **C** and **D** from a pamphlet on slavery. In British ports like Liverpool and Bristol, merchants would fit out specially built ships called slavers. They would carry a cargo of goods, such as looking-glasses, glass necklaces and knives, to swap for slaves. The slave boat would sail to West Africa, where the captain would anchor off the coast and buy a cargo of slaves from a local trader:

> *The price of a boy slave at Sierra Leone, seven fifty-pound kettles, five pieces of cloth, one piece of ramal and one bar of iron …*
> *The price of a man slave at Affinee, eight trading guns, one whicker bottle, two cases of spirits, twenty-eight sheets.* **(A)**

A slave ship. What ideas about slavery do you think the artist was trying to get across?

The slaves, **B**, were crammed in the hold of the boat:

> *Q. Were they then closely packed, or had they room sufficient to lie in comfort?*
> *A. They had not so much room as a man has in his coffin neither in length or breadth, and it was impossible for them to turn or shift with any degree of ease. I have had occasion very often to go from one side of their rooms to the other; before I attempted it I have always taken off my shoes, notwithstanding I have trod [upon them].* **(C)**

(Evidence to a parliamentary enquiry, 1790)

The voyage from Africa to America took around two months. Below deck, rows of Negroes lived in squalor. The stench was awful as very little fresh air got in through the gratings in the deck. The slave decks were swilled out with sea water once or twice a week. The chained slaves were brought on deck in batches to exercise - can you think why? Food was a foul maize gruel. Disease was the slavers' greatest fear - it could sweep through the entire ship.

> *We recommend to you to make fires frequently in the Negroe rooms, as we think it healthy and you have iron kettles on board for that purpose. We recommend mutton broth in fluxes, so that you endeavour to purchase as many sheep and goats to bring off the Coast for that purpose.* **(D)**

(A ship's orders, 1774)

In America and the West Indies the slaves were sold at a slave market and sent to work on sugar or cotton farms. By the 1780s slavery and the slave trade were under fierce attack in Britain. People such as William Wilberforce led the attack. In 1807 Parliament banned the British slave trade and in 1833 all British slaves were freed. Until then many people had been in favour of slavery - can you think why?

The Slave Trade Game

The map for this game is on page 96.

To enlarge the game you need **three** sets of 'chance cards' for squares C1, C2 and C3. There should be four cards for each topic, showing what might happen on the voyage:
• the trip from Bristol to West Africa and the buying of slaves
• the passage from Africa to Jamaica and the selling of slaves
• the return voyage to Bristol.

1 The cards (AT1)
• Do research for your chance cards. The cards should show what might happen on your voyage.
• See how small a space you can pack your class into - in two head-to-head rows, with a metre gap between them for the crew to walk down.
• Then play the game.

2 Introduction (AT2, AT1)
To tell the players what slavery was about, produce a 100-word introduction to the game in the form of a story about a voyage on the *Africa* in 1774, and a slave sale poster. Think about designing posters for selling members of your class as slaves.

3 Use **A-D** to help you write or mime the story of a slave of your own age. Mention: life in Africa; capture; the trip to the coast; sale to a slaver; chains; the ship's hold; the voyage - food, exercise, death, smells, tastes; Jamaica; the slave auction.

The Game

October 1774. Bristol. You are the captain of a slave ship, the *Africa*, which is about to set sail to Bonny on the slave coast. There it will pick up a cargo of slaves and ivory and sail to Jamaica. In Jamaica, the *Africa* will sell its slaves at the slave market and you will return to Bristol with a cargo of sugar.

How well would you do as a slave ship captain on this voyage? To see, use the map on page 96 and the rules below; the table shows you what happens on different dice numbers.

Rules
a Up to four people can take part.
b You will need a dice, four (small) counters and pencil and paper.
c Take turns in alphabetical order of your surnames.
d Keep a record of what happens to you as you go along.
e On your go place your counter, which represents your ship, on the Bristol square.
• Throw the dice and move your ship the number of squares or areas the dice shows, in any direction you want.
• Your aim is to reach Bonny on the slave coast.
• When you land on a 'chance square', turn up a card and do what it says.
• Then place the card face down at the bottom of the pack.

f When you reach Bonny, throw the dice to see what you can buy - see column 2 of the table below.
g Now start your journey to Jamaica. When you reach it, throw the dice to see what has happened to your cargo of slaves and how much money you have made (columns 3 and 4).
h Now return to Bristol.
i The winner is the player who makes the most money.

Dice number	Slaves bought	Slaves died	Price for each slave sold
1	200	20	£28
2	220	30	£30
3	240	40	£31
4	260	60	£32
5	280	80	£34
6	300	100	£36

THE MAP FOR THIS GAME IS ON PAGE 96

War of Independence

The Boston Tea Party

How often have people in your class moved to a new area? From the time of the Pilgrim Fathers, thousands of families left Britain to go and live in the British colonies in North America. Slowly these settlers pushed back the frontier, fought the native Indians, cleared the land for farming and built farms, villages and towns, **D**.

From 1775 to 1781, Britain's 13 American colonies fought a fierce war to break away from Britain. In 1776 the colonies issued their Declaration of Independence. The **causes** of the war were many and complex. To me the major reason was that Americans wanted to run their own affairs and did not see why they had to be ruled from Britain.

During the war the campaigns were an awful muddle, with well-trained British armies of redcoats fighting a guerilla army of colonists. George Washington commanded the American army. Neither side was able to win the land war. It only came to an end after 1778 because the French fleet cut off the British army in North America from Britain, and forced it to surrender, **B**.

After the war Washington became America's first president. The new America was made up of **states** (the old colonies). Each state ran its own internal affairs. The President was in charge of the army and foreign affairs.

In the nineteenth century America boomed and grew as the frontier was pushed further and further west, and America had its own Industrial Revolution. By 1900 the USA was the world's richest country. Britain's gain of a new empire in the East, based upon India, balanced the loss of her 13 American colonies.

FACTFILE

B

Date	Event
1632-1732	Britain builds up its American colonies. They become rich by farming and trade, and develop large towns and ports like Boston and New York.
1756-63	The Seven Years' War. Britain defeats France and seizes her colonies of Canada, Florida and the West Indies.
1765-73	The British government tries to tax the Americans to pay for the cost of the Seven Years' War. Colonists protest bitterly and riot against paying new taxes.
1773	The **Tea Act** forces colonists to pay a high price for tea. Boston Tea Party - colonists dressed as Red Indians dump a load of tea into Boston harbour. (I always like to use **A** to teach about the Boston Tea Party.)
1774	Britain closes Boston harbour. Colonies meet to plan joint action.
1775	**18 April.** The British get ready to send troops to seize arms and supplies at Concord. Paul Revere and others ride through the night to warn the colonists. Next day, when the British march, armed colonists wait for them. At Lexington and Concord fighting breaks out - the war has begun.
1775-77	Under Washington, the rebel army fights hard against the British. Often close to defeat, Washington keeps his army intact. At Valley Forge his army spends a bitter, cold winter in tents, **C**, facing British attacks. (I chose **C** because it is so vivid.) By **1778** the British campaigns have failed although Washington has never been able to beat the British army in a pitched battle.
1778	France declares war on Britain. The French fleet cut off the British army from home.
1781	Washington and a French army force the British to surrender at Yorktown.
1783	Peace is signed, and America becomes an independent country.

Catalogue

You have to prepare a catalogue entry for picture **A** to interest a 10-year-old.

1 The entry (AT2)
Write the entry from **either** the British **or** the American point of view. Give the picture a caption, put in speech bubbles from the mouths of people in the picture and add a four-sentence story of what the picture shows.

2 Storytime (AT1)
Use **A-C** and map **D** to h
a story about an Americaı
took part in both scenes.
Mention why the war bro
and the struggle that follo

ACTIVITY · ACTIVITY

C

D

CANADA · Great Lakes

Quebec
Montreal

Boston · Halifax

New York
Philadelphia

Jamestown

THE THIRTEEN COLONIES
· Charleston

Atlantic Ocean

New Orleans

WEST INDIES

The Indian Mutiny

Key
— Main roads
0   200 Miles

Thousands of tongues spread the rumour that swept through the market-places of India. The Indians would drive the British out of India, 100 years after Plassey.

In 1857 the British had cause to fear. Britain had kicked out India's old rulers and they were itching to win back their kingdoms. Also, Indian troops in the British army were on the edge of revolt. The 300,000 Indian soldiers, called *sepoys*, were mainly Hindus. They feared that the British would force them to become Christians. Then their Hindu souls would be damned. The cartridges for their new rifles confirmed their fears. They would have to bite off the end of the cartridge, which was smeared with grease. If the grease was from a cow they would be eating their most sacred animal; if it was from a pig they would be guilty of eating an unclean animal.

Britain's 40,000 white troops were scattered in small garrisons across northern India. The main fighting force was on the north-west frontier, **A**. In May the sepoys at Meerut, a British army base, rose in revolt and slaughtered the Europeans in the town. The rising spread to Delhi, which soon fell into rebel hands. From June to August the British lost control of the north Indian plain and their garrisons, and soldiers and their families were killed, retreated or were besieged, **B**. At Cawnpore the Indians massacred all the British. Many of the old Indian ruling families led the rising. One famous Indian leader I thought might interest you was a woman - the ruler, or *Rani*, of Jhansi, **C**.

The Rani of Jhansi

Using loyal troops the British fought a long, slow campaign to win back control. Fighting was bloody and fierce and the British butchered Indians in huge numbers, as I think painting **D** suggests. A British army retook Jhansi. This

Indian's story of what happened when the slaughter stopped moved me:

> 66 *In the squares of the city the sepoys and soldiers collected hundreds of corpses in large heaps and covered them with wood, floorboards and anything that came handy and set them on fire. Now every square blazed with burning bodies and the city looked like a vast burning ground... It became difficult to breathe as the air stank with the stench of the burning human flesh and the stink of rotting animals in the streets.* 99 **(E)**

(Anon, 1858)

The Rani fled but was killed later, while fighting with her troops. Today she is thought of in India as their Joan of Arc - can you think why?

The Indian Mutiny came to an end in 1859. The British government took full control over the country. Before this they had ruled through a private company, the East India Company. In 1876 Queen Victoria became Empress of India. Indians call the Indian Mutiny their 'First War of Independence'. Why?

Researching a story

I learnt about the Indian Mutiny from reading a novel. You can write a story about the mutiny from the point of view of **either** an Indian **or** a British person of your age.

1 Prepare your notes (AT3, AT1)
Use these headings to help you:
• living in Meerut; the rising starts; reasons
• to Delhi; risings; battles and the Cawnpore massacre
• Jhansi and the Rani; Jhansi falls; massacre of Indians in the town
• the Rani's flight and death; ideas about her.
Include a map or dateline in your notes.

2 The story (AT2, AT1)
Decide on the form your story will take. You can choose the approach you think best, such as a spy report, a young person's adventure or a diary. You can include drawings or copies of pictures **C** and **D** with your own captions.

ACTIVITY · ACTIVITY ·

B	FACTFILE

Date	Event
1856	The British take full control of the province of Oudh, including the capital, Lucknow. Indian sepoys protest strongly against the new cartridges for their rifles.
1857	**10 May.** Massacre at Meerut; fall of Delhi to rebels. **May–June.** Rising spreads across northern India. **June.** Rebels besiege Lucknow. **July.** Massacre of the British at Cawnpore. **July.** British begin to win back control over northern India. **September.** Delhi recaptured; Lucknow relieved, but besieged again. **November.** Lucknow relieved; British retreat from the city. **December.** Battle of Cawnpore; main rebel army routed.
1858	**January–March.** Campaign to win back Lucknow and the Ganges plain. **21 March.** Lucknow recaptured; Indian forces defeated on all fronts. **3 April.** Jhansi stormed; Rani escapes. **June.** Rani killed fighting the British. **July–December.** Bands of rebels wiped out throughout northern India.
1859	**April.** Capture and execution of the last rebel leader.

D

The Scramble for Africa

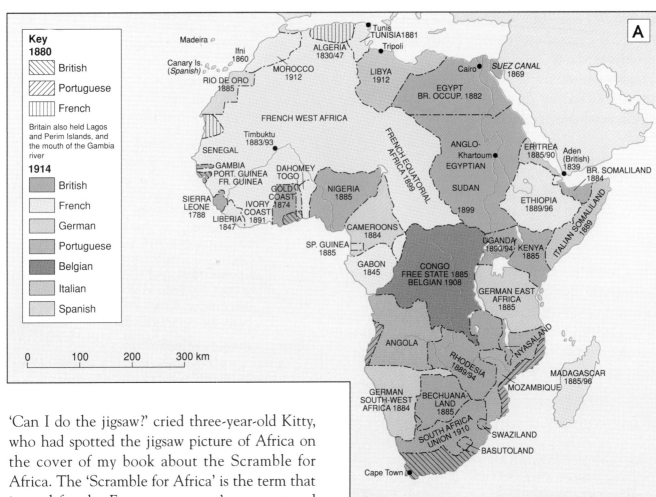

Key
1880

- ⬚ British
- ⬚ Portuguese
- ⬚ French

Britain also held Lagos and Perim Islands, and the mouth of the Gambia river

1914

- ⬚ British
- ⬚ French
- ⬚ German
- ⬚ Portuguese
- ⬚ Belgian
- ⬚ Italian
- ⬚ Spanish

0   100   200   300 km

'Can I do the jigsaw?' cried three-year-old Kitty, who had spotted the jigsaw picture of Africa on the cover of my book about the Scramble for Africa. The 'Scramble for Africa' is the term that is used for the European powers' conquest and carving up of Africa between them after 1875.

In 1875 Africa was a land of Negro tribes under their own chiefs, and a haunt of missionaries, explorers and traders. The most famous missionary was Dr Livingstone, who met Henry Stanley, a reporter, on the banks of Lake Tanganyika. 'Dr Livingstone, I presume?' was Stanley's famous remark.

By 1875 explorers had seen most of Africa, and European countries had trading posts on the African coast, **A**. In South Africa the British had seized a Dutch colony during the Napoleonic Wars, to supply ships on the way to India. So the British ruled the area around Cape Town, while Dutch settlers, the Boers, had trekked inland and had founded the Transvaal and the Orange Free State, **B**.

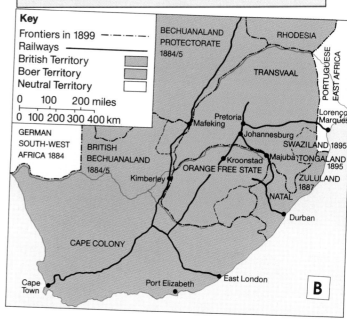

Key
- Frontiers in 1899 — — —
- Railways ———
- British Territory ⬚
- Boer Territory ⬚
- Neutral Territory ⬚

0   100   200 miles
0 100 200 300 400 km

The Scramble for Africa began after Belgium claimed the Congo in 1875. In **1884**, at Berlin, the powers of Europe decided to carve up Africa between them. They drew lines on the map without any idea of what Africa was like. Looking at **A** and **B**, can you work out which colonies had parts of their boundaries drawn with a ruler - so cutting regions and tribes in half? Today these boundaries are those of modern African countries.

• Britain gained the **Gold Coast, Nigeria, Uganda, Kenya** and **Bechuanaland** - largely to keep out the French and Germans but also for trading purposes.

• Britain seized **Somaliland** to control the Red Sea route to India.

• Britain also seized **Egypt** to protect the route to India through the Suez Canal.

• Control over Egypt brought problems, because Egypt ruled the **Sudan.** In 1885 the Mahdi, a religious fanatic, raised an army of Dervishes who attacked Khartoum and killed General Gordon, the British governor. In 1898 a British army marched into the Sudan, slaughtered the Dervishes at the Battle of Omdurman and added the Sudan to the British Empire.

• In **South Africa** the British and the Boers lived in peace until the 1870s, when the discovery of gold and diamonds on Boer land led to a rush of foreign settlers to the gold-fields. In the next 20 years fighting broke out between the native Zulus, the Boers and the British over who should rule the area.

Cecil Rhodes, an Englishman and the richest diamond miner, wanted Britain to rule all South Africa. Rhodes even hoped for a British railway from the Cape to Cairo, **C**. He claimed Bechuanaland for Britain, and in 1893 Rhodes smashed the army of the African ruler of Rhodesia and joined that area to the British Empire. In 1899 Britain and the Boers went to war, the Boer War, over Britain's claim to rule the Boers. Britain finally won. During the Scramble for Africa no-one asked the Africans what they thought. What might they have said?

C

Jigsaw

You can design and make your own 'Imperial Jigsaw' of Africa for a three-year-old, like Kitty, to play with. Work on your own or in pairs.

1 Design (AT1)
Decide what your jigsaw will look like. Copy **A** on to thick paper or card. Include the names of the colonies and, where known, their dates.

2 Finding out (AT3, AT1)
Read this chapter to find out how Britain gained colonies in Africa before 1900. Then:

• Colour in the British colonies according to what you think they were gained for.

colour	reason
black	trade (before 1875)
red	gold and diamonds
blue	protect the trade route to India
yellow	keep out the French
green	keep out the Germans

• On each colony put the name of the modern country.

3 Notes (AT2, AT1)
Now you have your jigsaw, you need to provide notes and a map to go with it. In 100 words, write an account of how Europe colonised Africa. On an outline map show the colonies by 1875, and the land in European hands in 1900.

ACTIVITY · ACTIVITY ·

The French Revolution

In 1989 a huge row broke out. The British Prime Minister, Margaret Thatcher, went to France to help celebrate the 200th anniversary of the French Revolution. In Paris she told the French that the English Civil War of 1642-49 and the 'Glorious Revolution' of 1688 had done more for freedom for the people than the French Revolution of 1789. The French were very angry, because they said that it was the French Revolution that had first brought freedom for ordinary people. What was their revolution about?

• Before 1789 the **French king** had ruled France from his palace at **Versailles.**

• The **French clergy and nobles** paid little tax and the main burden fell on the **peasants**. Two of the worst taxes were a land tax, the *taille*, and a tax to pay for mending the roads, the *corvée*. **A** is one of my favourite cartoons about this - can you work out its message?

• In 1789 the **French king was broke**, mainly because of what it had cost him to fight in the American War of Independence, see page 77.

• **The king called a meeting of the old French Parliament**, the **Estates General**, to help him raise cash. The Estates General was made up of three groups or estates: nobles; clergy; and the third estate of peasants, lawyers, bankers, merchants and civil servants.

• **The third estate** told the king that it must have a say in government in return for finding him the money he needed to rule.

Crowds on the streets of Paris backed the third estate, and in July 1789 they stormed the king's main fort in Paris, the Bastille, **B**. In August the mob forced the king to leave his huge palace at Versailles, just outside Paris, to come and live in the capital. The king was really a prisoner, and the French Revolution had begun. Its slogan was 'Freedom, equality and brotherhood'.

A

The leaders of the French Revolution became France's new rulers. They accused the king, Louis XVI, of plotting with their enemies to overthrow them and tried him for treason. Louis was found guilty and executed in January 1793. Thousands of nobles and clergy followed him to the guillotine during a period known as 'The Terror'. By now France was at war with most of Europe and fighting to keep her territory. Soon a new French leader would emerge from her army - Napoleon Bonaparte.

Revolutionary Postcards

What thoughts might a rich, conservative, British landowner and a supporter of the American Revolution have had if they had been in France at the storming of the Bastille? You can design a postcard to show the fall of the Bastille, and write a message on it.

1 Research (AT3, AT1)
Find out as much as you can about the start of the French Revolution and the storming of the Bastille.
• Note three facts about **A**. Work out the message you think the artist was trying to get across and what light it might throw on the outbreak of the French Revolution.
• What impression does picture **B** give?
• What thoughts might be going through the minds of any three people in **B**?

2 Your postcard (AT2)
Design your own postcard, showing the fall of the Bastille. Then, as if you were in Paris at the time and were **either** the rich, conservative, British landowner **or** the supporter of the American Revolution, write a message of 50 words or more to your best friend telling him or her what is going on. Say what you think the slogan 'Freedom, equality and brotherhood' might mean, and what you feel about the French Revolution.

ACTIVITY · ACTIVITY

Napoleon

Ask your grandparents why the Home Guard, 'Dad's Army', was set up and what it did. About 200 years ago the first Home Guard, 'The Volunteers', was founded to fight as deadly an enemy as Hitler - Napoleon, ruler of France. In 1804 Napoleon became France's emperor, and planned to invade Britain. In your area the local squire, with army help, would have trained a local force of Volunteers to fight Napoleon. I found source **A** in an old textbook - no attempt here to give a balanced view - while **B** is based on an account I wrote 10 years ago. **C** is my favourite picture of him - can you think why I like it? **D** shows how Goya, the artist, felt about the way Napoleon's troops treated the Spanish.

66 *Louis XVI and his unhappy queen, Marie Antoinette, were guillotined, and the* **Reign of Terror** *followed. The Republicans promised aid to any country that would rise against their monarchs. Out of this social chaos, there arose the most remarkable man known in European history,* **Napoleon Bonaparte**, *who shook the foundations of every empire, kingdom, and state of the continent. During a career of bloodshed and despotism, he re-organised the social life of his country, and remodelled its political institutions. Toulon, a royalist city, which had placed itself under the protection of Britain, was recaptured for the Republic by the cannon directed by this man, then in his youth, who here first distinguished himself as an artillery officer. He soon took the control of affairs into his own hands, and scattered the National Guard by a volley of grape shot, before the Palace of the Tuileries, 1795 – thus saving the French Directory from the assault of an infuriated mob. In 1796, he married Josephine Beauharnais, and, by her influence, he obtained command of the French army in Italy, and humbled the power of Austria and her allies.*

Events in Egypt.— *The French were very jealous of our power in the East, and in the year 1798 sent an army under Napoleon, into Egypt to reduce that country, so that they could make it useful in fighting against the English in India. He was successful in subduing the country, but the fleet that carried his army was almost completely destroyed at the battle of the Nile, in Aboukir Bay, by Admiral Nelson. After this, Bonaparte led his army across the desert into Palestine and besieged Acre, but it was bravely defended by Sir Sydney Smith, and he was compelled to retire. He then returned to France, without his army, and was made First Consul.* 99 **(A)**

(Roscoe Mongan, *The Oxford and Cambridge History of England*, 1904)

66 *In 1805 the English admiral, Horatio Nelson, defeated the French fleet at the battle of Trafalgar. Trafalgar meant the end of Napoleon's plans to invade Britain. It seemed he would conquer all of Europe instead. By 1811 he had beaten two of its great powers - Prussia (Germany) and Austria-Hungary (central Europe). In 1812 he made a fatal mistake when he tried to conquer Russia. Although he reached Moscow, he had to turn back. Most of his huge army died on the march. Europe's powers turned against him. In 1814 he was driven from France and forced to live in exile on the island of Elba. Europe seemed to be at peace, but in 1815 Napoleon returned to France. Quickly he raised an army, but at Waterloo in 1815 the Duke of Wellington and his ally, Blucher, the Prussian general, destroyed the French army. Napoleon was sent to live on St. Helena, a small island in the Atlantic, where he died.* 99 **(B)**

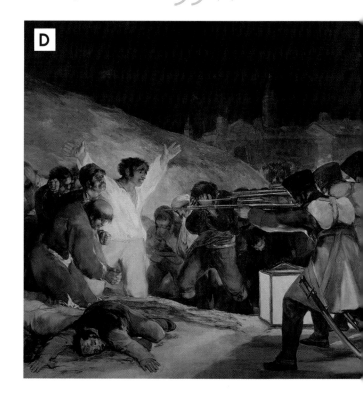

D

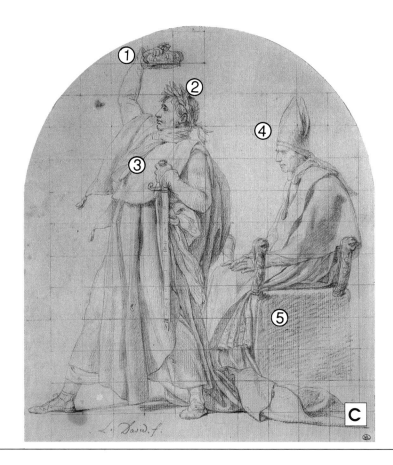

Handbill or History Dictionary

You can produce **either** a 'Wanted - dead or alive' poster for Napoleon after his return from Elba **or** a 100-word entry (biography) on Napoleon for a history dictionary for 10-year-olds. Use the biographical headings below to help you. Find out all you can from books about him.

BIOGRAPHICAL HEADINGS

NAME ....

FACTFILE

a Key dates:

b Facts and information:
- What was he like as a person?
- Why did he matter?
- What were the reasons or motives for his actions?
- What were the results of his actions?

---

1 Research - finding out and thinking about Napoleon (AT3)

• Read **quickly** through **A** and **B**. Jot down the key ideas they give about Napoleon. For each source, what is the author's point of view?

• Read **A** and **B slowly** and note what seem to be important dates and events. Under each **biographical heading** put down the information that **A** and **B** convey.

• Look at **C**. What ideas did Napoleon want you to have about him? Study points 1-5 on the picture to find out.

• Study **D** in detail. Close your eyes and think about any ideas and thoughts the picture gives you. Think of titles for **C** and **D**, and add any ideas you get from them to the information under your biographical headings.

• Find out all you can about Napoleon, Wellington, Trafalgar and Waterloo. Put down your findings under the correct biographical headings.

2 The biography (AT1, AT2)

• Use the headings and your notes to write your biography from a neutral, pro- or anti-Napoleon stance.

• You can put in a cartoon, and a poster to get people to join **either** the Volunteers **or** a force supporting the French invasion.

• Read out or display the biographies around the class. Pick out the best one.

ACTIVITY · ACTIVITY ·

The Great Reform Bill

At Peterloo in 1819, Orator Hunt had demanded changes in the way MPs were chosen. The result was a massacre, see page 49. Yet within 13 years the Government had pushed through the **Great Reform Bill**, which brought about much of what Hunt had wanted. Why? How? My history books said that there were four main **causes**:

1 The old system of election before 1832 seemed crazy, see **A**. MPs were drawn from Britain's richest families of landowners, merchants and bankers. Most MPs sat for towns or boroughs, some of which were bought and sold. Voters often took bribes. Most boroughs were in the hands of local rich families, on whose land or in whose houses voters lived. There were a large number of seats in the south

and west of England. The Industrial Revolution meant that this pattern became more and more out of step with where people were living, see **B**.

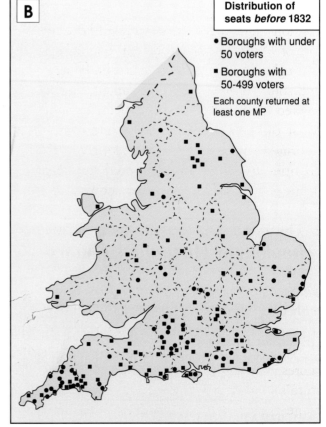

B Distribution of seats *before* 1832

- Boroughs with under 50 voters
- Boroughs with 50-499 voters

Each county returned at least one MP

FACTFILE

A

The House of Commons
- **Before 1832** the House of Commons had 558 members, 489 for England.
- The seats split into two main kinds - county seats; city and borough seats.

Counties
- Counties chose two MPs each, 80 in all.
- In the counties, anyone owning land worth £2 had the vote.
- There was a large electorate in the counties - with an average of around 4,000 per county.

Cities and Boroughs
- The cities and boroughs had one or two MPs each (405), with four for Oxford and Cambridge universities.
- Boroughs had an amazing range of voting rights - with quaint names like Scot and Lot and Potwalloper - from being born a freeman, to owning a house plot, or to the corporation (town council) having the right to choose the MPs.
- The number of voters per borough varied enormously. The average was about 1000. About one man in 20 had the right to vote.
- Some boroughs had no inhabitants - Old Sarum was a hill and Dunwich was under the sea!
- MPs had to look after their towns and their voters - find them jobs, make sure the trade and

industry of the town were protected, and get Acts of Parliament passed, when needed, for things like building bridges and turnpike roads, paving the town, and putting in a water works.

- Voting took place in public, in both county and borough elections.
- **In 1761**, 111 peers and commoners - mostly rich landowners - decided, or had a strong say in, the choice of 195 MPs.

The 1832 Reform Bill
- **In 1832**, voting rights were given in **boroughs** to male owners of houses worth £10 rent a year; in **counties** to owners of land worth £2, or tenants paying £10 rent a year for long leases over 21 years and £50 rent a year for short leases. Each county got an extra seat and Yorkshire got two.

2 Catholic Emancipation. In 1828 Catholics were hated in England - can you think why? English Catholics neither had the vote nor could they become MPs. But in Ireland, a Catholic was chosen as an MP. The Government knew that if it tried to deny him his seat in Parliament, civil war would break out. So the Government had to give Catholics the vote and the right to sit in Parliament - Catholic Emancipation - against the wishes of most of England's MPs.

Catholic Emancipation was passed because lots of MPs who sat for 'rotten' boroughs - boroughs where the seats could be bought and sold - backed the Government, and it looked as if these MPs had been bribed. Most of the rest of the MPs felt that a reformed Parliament - with seats given to counties and large towns - would stop any future government sell-out and betrayal.

3 The middle-class and working-class alliance. In cities like Birmingham and Leeds, the middle-class factory owners, shopkeepers and businessmen joined forces with the workers to press for parliamentary reform. They felt it was a nonsense that their towns and cities had no MPs to represent their interests. Political Unions were set up to push for reform. They held huge marches and rallies and the Government feared there might be a revolution.

4 Economic crisis. In 1829 Britain plunged into a major recession. The results were the Swing Riots of 1830, see pages 50-51.

A **Reform Bill** was introduced in 1830. It took two years to pass, during which there were major riots in towns that were backing reform. The bill shared out seats in a much fairer way than before, **C**. The bill made sure that the boroughs' boundaries took in all the town and enough of the land around it to **represent the local community**. Voting rights were given to men who owned **property**, see factfile **A**.

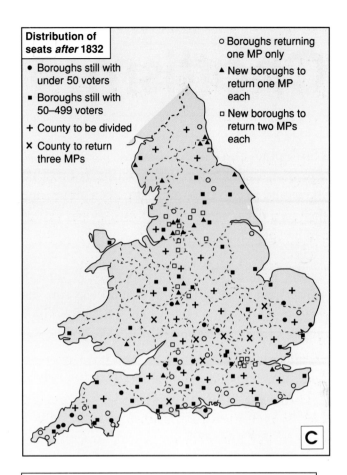

Distribution of seats after 1832

- ● Boroughs still with under 50 voters
- ■ Boroughs still with 50–499 voters
- + County to be divided
- × County to return three MPs
- ○ Boroughs returning one MP only
- ▲ New boroughs to return one MP each
- □ New boroughs to return two MPs each

C

Electoral Reform

You have to draw or plan a cartoon or picture to be used with a school radio programme on the Reform Bill. The plan or cartoon will show the causes of the bill - why it was needed.

1 Finding out (AT3, AT1)
If you can, work out from old textbooks a timechart of the passing of the Reform Bill from 1830-32. Study the text and sources **A-C**. Decide if in 1832 each of these:
- The old electoral system
- Catholic Emancipation
- The Political Unions
- The economic crisis of 1829-32
Was:
a) a long term cause of reform?
b) a short term cause of reform?
c) a major cause?
d) a minor cause?
Give reasons for your choice.

2 Drawing or cartoon (AT2, AT1)
Your drawing, cartoon or plan should include points about the old electoral system, Catholic Emancipation, the Political Unions and the economic crisis.

ACTIVITY ACTIVITY

Chartism

Think of all the things you don't like about the way your school is run. Jot down six points that you would like to have put right. As a group, and then as a class, agree on a list of six ideas. These can be your charter.

In the mid-1830s many leaders of groups of workers did not like the way Britain was run and the way that MPs were chosen. They drew up a charter to bring about reform. Their charter demanded:

- Manhood suffrage (all men to have the vote)
- Pay for Members of Parliament
- MPs not to have to own land to become a Member of Parliament
- Vote by secret ballot
- Electoral districts to have the same number of voters
- Parliaments to be elected each year.

Across Britain local movements sprang up to back the charter. Three times - in 1839, 1842 and 1848 - the Chartists marched to Parliament with a vast petition, **A**. Each time Parliament threw it out, although in time the first five demands became law. There were several reasons why the charter got huge support:

- The 1832 Reform Bill had not given working-

class men the vote
- The Poor Law Amendment Act of 1834 made the poor much worse off than they had been before
- The idea of votes for all men had a wide appeal
- There were bad harvests, high prices and industrial depressions in the mid-1830s, in 1840-41 and in 1846-47
- Chartists believed that social reform would follow the reform of Parliament.

Chartist Seance

1 Chartist ideas (AT1, AT3)
- Write out the charter's points, and alongside the first five say why the Government thinks each is a good idea now but opposed it in the 1830s and 1840s.
- What message does **A** try to get across about the Chartists and the problems they faced?

2 The seance (AT3, AT2)
At a seance, if you were able to speak to the following Chartists, what might they say was their main reason for backing the charter?

- Thomas Attwood, a Birmingham banker and Chartist leader
- Francis Place, a London radical who had played a big part in the campaign to reform Parliament before 1832
- Shropshire coal miners, whose wages were cut in 1841
- An out-of-work handloom weaver with a wife and five children, who are all about to enter the workhouse.

The Irish Famine

Six famished and ghastly skeletons, to all appearance dead, huddled in a corner. Their sole covering was what seemed to be a ragged horse cloth, and their wretched legs hanging about, naked above the knees. I approached in horror and found by a low moaning that they were alive. They were in a fever - four children, a woman and what had once been a man. The doctor found seven wretches lying, unable to move, under the same cloak. One had been dead many hours, but the others were unable to move... in a few minutes I was surrounded by at least 200 such phantoms, such frightful spectres as no words can describe, either from famine or fever. Their demoniac [devilish] yells are still ringing in my ears... **(A)**

(Letter from an Irish JP to the Duke of Wellington, printed in *The Times*, 1847)

I was woken in the early morning by a strange noise, like the croaking or chattering of many birds. Some of the voices were hoarse and almost gone by the faintness of famine. On looking out of the window I remember seeing the garden and the field in front of the house darkened by a huge crowd of men, women and children. They squatted in rags, uncovered skeleton limbs poked out everywhere from their wretched clothing. And clamorous though faint voices rose up for food. **(B)**

(Memories of Josephine Butler, aged 13)

News reports from Africa? Today radio, TV and newspapers bring horror stories like **A-C** into all our homes. About 150 years ago the Government let the same thing happen to Britons living in Ireland.

A book that moved me deeply was Cecil Woodham-Smith's *The Great Famine*, an account of the Irish Famine of 1846-47. I picked **A** and **B** out of it - I always use these in my teaching - and I found **C** to use with them. **E** is a scene in Skibbereen, the village talked about in **A**. Factfile **D** should help you make sense of the famine, while **F** and **G** will help build up the picture of what the Irish Famine meant.

A disease called potato blight caused the Irish Famine, because blight killed the potato on

C

which the people lived. With no food to be had, many starved to death or sailed away in hope to England or America. Ireland's population dropped from about seven million to five million. The British government had failed to feed the dying Irish. The Irish have never forgiven, or forgotten, what they think of as the mass murder of their people.

In the 1840s, Ireland was still a country of dirt tracks where life moved at the pace of a walking man or a horse. I came across quotation **H**, which gave me some idea of what Ireland was like then.

FACTFILE

D

• Ireland was a British colony. Ireland's history tells of many attempts to break free from the British grip. Before 1920 all attempts failed.

• In the seventeenth century many English, Welsh and Scots went to live or settled in Northern Ireland. The settlers were mainly Protestants, the native Irish were Catholics.

• Risings of the Catholic Irish failed during the English Civil War, 1642-49, and in 1688-90. The Catholics were finally crushed at the Battle of the Boyne in 1690, and much of their remaining land was taken from them.

• During the time of the American War of Independence, both Catholics and Protestants in Ireland pushed for the right to run their own affairs. In 1782 the Irish Parliament was given much more power.

• At the time of the French Revolution the British government feared that the Irish would revolt against them, with French support. In 1798 the Irish did rise and over 50,000 died in a bloody war.

• In 1801 the Act of Union killed off the Irish Parliament and Ireland was ruled from London. In return, Ireland sent 80 MPs to the House of Commons.

• Although Irish Catholics who owned property worth 40 shillings a year in tax could vote, they could not sit in Parliament.

• In the late 1820s a Catholic, Daniel O'Connell, fought this ban and stood as an MP. When he was chosen the British government felt that it had to allow him to take his seat. Otherwise there would have been a civil war.

• In 1829 Parliament granted Catholic Emancipation.

• 1845. Outbreaks of potato blight in Ireland.

• 1846-47. The Irish Famine.

• Today the split between Protestants and Catholics still divides Northern Ireland, where the Catholic IRA is fighting a bitter guerilla war against the British.

E

. SMYTH

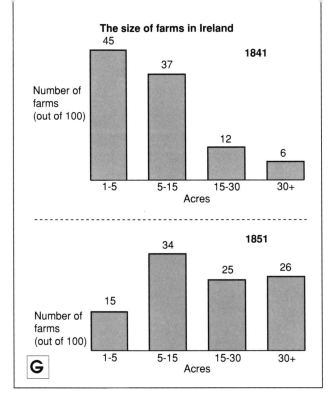

The size of farms in Ireland

1841

1851

G

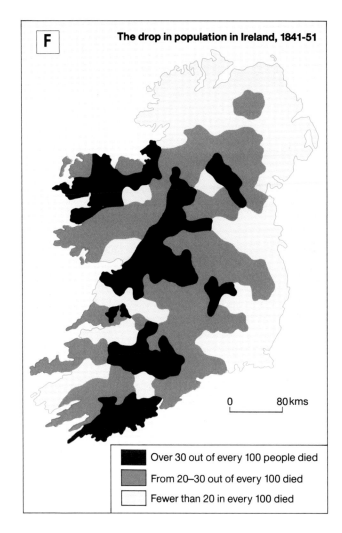

F **The drop in population in Ireland, 1841-51**

0   80 kms

■ Over 30 out of every 100 people died
▒ From 20–30 out of every 100 died
□ Fewer than 20 in every 100 died

There were almost no industries, there were very few towns, there were very few farms large enough to employ labour. The country was a country of holdings so small as to be mere patches. The people lived in huts of mud mingled with a few stones, huts four or five feet high built on the bare earth, roofed with boughs and turf sods without chimneys or windows and empty of furniture, where animals and human beings slept together on the mud floor... The people lacked land, tools and barns. Potatoes need only one third the acreage of wheat, grow anywhere, can be stored in the ground, shared with fowls and pigs... The Irish came to live on the 'Lumper' or 'Horse Potato'... Over great tracts of Ireland any form of cooking beyond boiling a potato in a pot became unknown. **(H)**

(C.Woodham-Smith, *The Reason Why*)

Famine

You can prepare the story lines and reports for a video documentary on the Irish Famine. You can include a one-side hand-out of information to go with the documentary.

1 The story (AT1, AT3)
• Choose a title.
• Talk about famine in the world today. Describe what you might see now on a visit to an area where people like those in **A** live.
• Travel back in time. Say what Ireland was like in 1846. Mention: farming; the size of farms, **G**; the role of the potato.

2 Report from Skibbereen (AT1, AT2, AT3)
Report on the state of Skibbereen in 1847.
• Describe a visit to a hut like the one in **C**. Say what you saw, heard and smelled.
• Interview one of the figures in **C** and one in **E**.

Ask them both these questions:
What happened to the potato harvest last year?
What has happened to the villagers since?
Who are the two people on the cart in **E**?
Why are they dressed in that way?

3 The impact of the Irish Famine (AT1)
Use **F** and **G** to say what the impact of the famine was. Why did the people die in the areas shown? What does the change in farm size suggest about the famine?

4 Famine relief (AT1)
In the 1840s, Ireland was a country of dirt tracks and horse transport. There were no railways and modern roads, and no modern medical services or medicines. Work out a plan for famine relief in 1846-47.

ACTIVITY · ACTIVITY

Reform 1867-1885

How would you feel if you were told today that you would not be getting the vote at 18? Or, if you had the vote, how would you feel if your boss or landlord told you which candidate to vote for?

Before 1867 most men did not have the vote. Also, because of the system of voting in public, those who could vote often had no chance to vote as they would have liked. Can you think why? The activity in this chapter helps you carry out a public opinion poll to see how people might have reacted in 1867 to plans being put forward to change the way the country was run.

In 1867 Parliament passed the **Second Reform Bill**, see factfile **A**. From 1867, something like the two-party system we know today grew up. But then the parties were Conservative and Liberal instead of Conservative and Labour. After 1868 the two party leaders were Gladstone and Disraeli. They fought like cats and dogs. I like cartoon **B** because it suggests to me that things haven't changed much since! In 1872 the **Secret Ballot** was introduced and in 1884-85 a **Third Reform Bill** was passed. This handed out seats more fairly than before and gave most skilled working men the vote. Women had to wait another 30 years before they could vote in parliamentary elections.

'DOCTORS DIFFER!'
Dr William G. 'I warn you, Mr. Bull, your constitution is being seriously impaired by that – a – person's treatment.'
Dr Benjamin D. 'My dear Mr. Bull, your constitution is perfectly safe in my hands.'

PUNCH, June 1, 1878

FACTFILE

A			
Date	Event	Date	Event
1867	**Reform Bill** • In towns and cities, all householders plus lodgers paying £10 rent a year get the vote. • In the counties, the vote goes to ratepayers paying £12 a year and to landowners with land worth £5 rent a year. • Towns with fewer than 10,000 voters lose one seat. • 45 seats are redistributed - 25 to counties, 15 to towns and cities. • The number of voters doubles to almost 2.5 million. • Large towns and cities still have far too few MPs for the number of voters.	1872 1884 1885	**Secret Ballot** • Voters now vote in secret. **Parliamentary Reform Act** • This gives the vote to all householders in the counties, doubling the electorate to 5.7 million. **Redistribution Act** • This takes the seats away from towns with fewer than 15,000 inhabitants and leaves towns and cities with between 15,000-50,000 people with one MP. • 142 seats are redistributed. • Constituencies now begin to look more like they do today.

Political Reform

Briefing:
The Conservatives have spent nearly all of the last 20 years out of office, while the Liberals have enjoyed power.

The Liberals have the support of MPs from the towns and the Conservatives control the counties.

The Conservatives are furious because 4,000 voters, on average, choose each county MP, while only 1,500 choose each town or city MP.

Both parties back electoral reform - with the growth of the large towns and cities and a skilled and often well-educated class of workers, the old system can no longer be defended.

1 Opinion poll (AT1, AT2)
• **Read the briefing**, and then record how the two people below might have reacted to the list of questions. In 1867 these plans for changes to the way Parliament was chosen were being put forward.

• **Split into pairs**. One of you takes the role of the opinion pollster, the other takes the role of the Conservative or the Liberal. **Swap roles** - and political parties - when you have been through the questions once.

> **The Conservative:**
> A rich landowner, whose friend is the Conservative MP for the county.
>
> **The Liberal:**
> A well-off shopkeeper, who has played a big part in setting up the local Liberal Party.

The vote in towns - 1
The Conservative Party has done very badly in the towns. Voters back the Liberals, whose policies seem to favour both industry and shopkeepers. Who might be helped by a huge increase in the voters? Should there be:
a Votes for all men paying over £30 rent a year? **or**
b Votes for all men paying over £20 rent a year? **or**
c Votes for all men paying over £10 rent a year?

The vote in towns - 2
The Conservatives have said that all house owners must be trusted to use the vote in a sensible way. Should there be:
a Votes for all male house owners? **or**
b Votes for all houses worth £50 a year in rates?

The vote in counties
The counties vote solidly Conservative. Should there be:
a Votes for houses paying over £54 a year in rates? **or**
b Votes for men paying £15 rent a year? **or**
c Votes for all men paying over £10 rent a year?

Places losing seats
The Conservatives are desperate to get more seats for county areas. Should:
a Towns with fewer than 5,000 people lose both seats? **or**
b Towns with fewer than 10,000 people lose one seat? **or**
c Towns with fewer than 15,000 people lose both seats? **or**
d Towns with fewer than 15,000 people lose one seat?

Places gaining seats - towns
Should:
a Towns with more than 50,000 people gain an extra seat? **or**
b Towns with between 50,000-165,000 people gain two seats?

Places gaining seats - counties
The more seats the merrier for the Conservatives! Should
a Counties get 25 new seats? **or**
b County areas get one new seat each?

Write out what your plan would be, and then compare it with your political opponent's plan.

Music Hall

Work out what you've done in the last 24 hours. How much time did you spend watching TV? What might you have done in an age where there was no TV or radio, no cassette or CD players, no videos or personal stereos? Here's a clue:

❝ *Imagine that it's a Saturday night in 1901, and you live in a narrow red-brick house with five brothers and three sisters and your Gran, in the East End of London, say Bethnal Green, and your Mum and Dad are looking forward to their favourite evening's entertainment. Can you guess what it is? It's not the latest spectacular on television, nor a James Bond film at the local cinema. It's not a Saturday night radio play, nor a session with the stereo music centre... [they weren't invented yet!].*

Well, what else is there? Perhaps you haven't guessed, because the answer doesn't really exist any more. But at the end of the last century and the beginning of this one, Music Hall was the most flourishing and popular entertainment for vast numbers of people... It was enjoyed mostly by working people, and it was not always thought respectable enough for men to take their wives. Its songs were the pop songs of the day, spread around by sales of song sheets, and errand boys' whistling... Music Hall stars were the pop stars of their day... Coming mostly from the working people, they were often vulgar, brash, colourful and very good at their job of keeping an extremely difficult audience amused. ❞ **(A)**

(Ann Purser, *Looking Back at Popular Entertainment, 1901-39*, 1978)

What might a visit to the Music Hall be like? After buying your ticket at the box office, you would enter a large theatre and take your seat - just like going to the cinema today. At the front there would be a small band or orchestra, and on the stage single acts or groups would take their turn. Lots of performers were young people of your age. The best-known of them all was Charlie Chaplin, who started his professional life as a clog dancer in a troupe of dancing boys. Acts would take many forms - from stand-up comics to jugglers, dancers and singers. Marie Lloyd, **B**, was a very famous Music Hall star.

B

Music Hall

You can plan your own Music Hall evening, and practise and perform your act.

1 Research and planning (AT3, AT1)
• Work out what kind of act you would like to present. It could be singing, reciting poems, miming, or telling jokes and stories.
• Make out a billboard to advertise the performance.

2 Presentation (AT1)
In turn, members of the class can present their acts or their ideas for acts.

3 The critic (AT2)
You have to produce a review of the show for your school magazine or newspaper. Tell the story of the night out and mention: getting ready to go out - thoughts and ideas; talking about Marie Lloyd - ideas you have of her from **B**; going into the theatre, the performers; the audience; and what you saw, heard and smelled.

ACTIVITY · ACTIVITY

A Trivial Pursuit?

At home we have 'Trivia for Kids' - a large box of cards like the one below. On one side of the cards there are six questions; on the other side, the answers. *Expansion, Trade and Industry* is packed with facts and information that you can turn into 'Trivia' questions to hold a class quiz or contest. This is also a good way of revising facts you will need for your **National History Tests**.

TRIVIA for KIDS™

1. In what country would you say "Sayonara" instead of "Goodbye"?
2. Which book and television character exclaims "Blistering Barnacles"?
3. What were the names of the ships of Columbus?
4. Where did Peter Pan live?
5. Who wrote "The Origin of the Species"?
6. Name the only Scottish football team to win the European Cup.

ANSWERS

1. Japan
2. Captain Haddock in Tin Tin
3. Nina, Pinta and Santa Maria
4. Never-Never-Land
5. Charles Darwin
6. Celtic

Trivia!

Using the information in this book, you can design your own 'Trivia' cards and then hold a class quiz.

1 Preparing the cards (AT3)
- As a class, split into two equal teams.
- Both teams are given the same list of topics to prepare 'Trivia' cards from.
- On the top of each card put the name of the topic, and then list six questions.
- On the back, put the six answers in the same order as the questions.

2 The contest (AT1)
- When the class has prepared its cards, the cards are collected in two separate piles and each pile is shuffled.
- The quiz organiser takes a card from team A's pile and asks team B the questions on it. Then he or she takes a card from team B's pile and asks team A the questions on it.
- One mark is awarded for a correct answer.
- The team with the highest score wins!

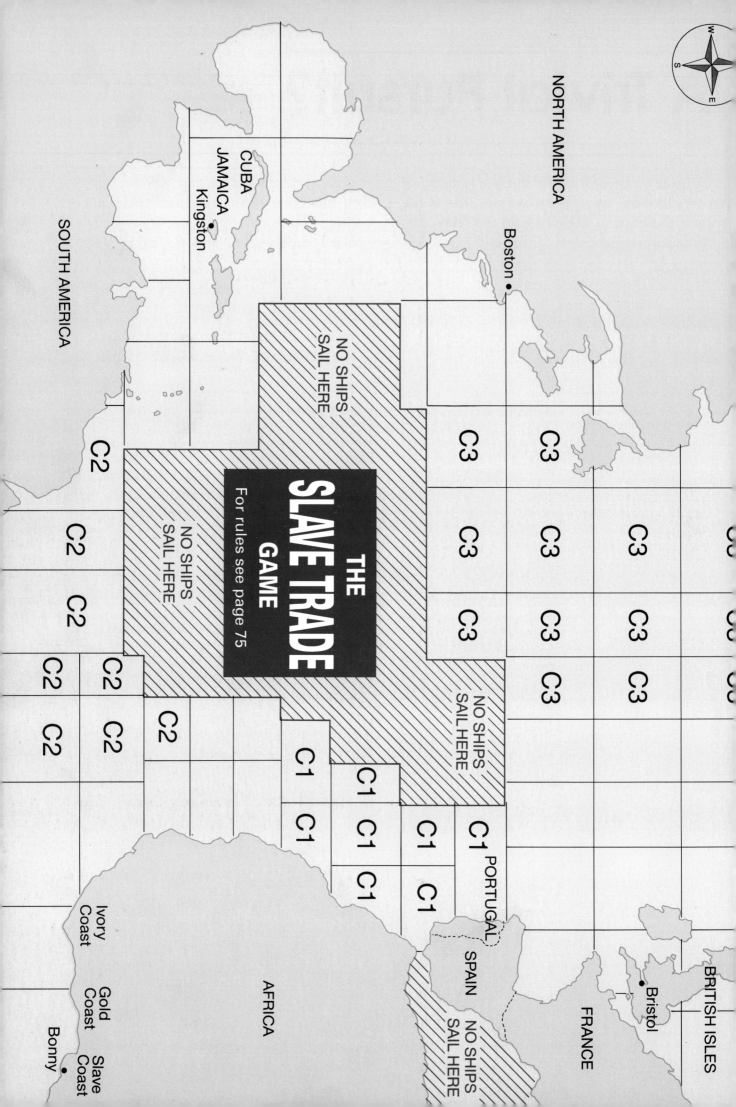